How To Publish Your Own Book

BOOKS BY VERNON COLEMAN

The Medicine Men (1975)
Paper Doctors (1976)
Everything You Want To Know About Ageing (1976)
Stress Control (1978)
The Home Pharmacy (1980)
Aspirin or Ambulance (1980)
Face Values (1981)
Guilt (1982)
The Good Medicine Guide (1982)
Stress And Your Stomach (1983)
Bodypower (1983)
An A to Z Of Women's Problems (1984)
Bodysense (1984)
Taking Care Of Your Skin (1984)
Life Without Tranquillisers (1985)
High Blood Pressure (1985)
Diabetes (1985)
Arthritis (1985)
Eczema and Dermatitis (1985)
The Story Of Medicine (1985, 1998)
Natural Pain Control (1986)
Mindpower (1986)
Addicts and Addictions (1986)
Dr Vernon Coleman's Guide To Alternative Medicine (1988)
Stress Management Techniques (1988)
Overcoming Stress (1988)
Know Yourself (1988)
The Health Scandal (1988)
The 20 Minute Health Check (1989)
Sex For Everyone (1989)
Mind Over Body (1989)
Eat Green Lose Weight (1990)
Toxic Stress (1991)
Why Animal Experiments Must Stop (1991)
The Drugs Myth (1992)
Why Doctors Do More Harm Than Good (1993)
Stress and Relaxation (1993)
Complete Guide to Sex (1993)
How to Conquer Backache (1993)
How to Conquer Arthritis (1993)
Betrayal of Trust (1994)
Know Your Drugs (1994, 1997)
Food for Thought (1994)
The Traditional Home Doctor (1994)
I Hope Your Penis Shrivels Up (1994)
People Watching (1995)
Relief from IBS (1995)
The Parent's Handbook (1995)

Oral Sex: Bad Taste And Hard To Swallow (1995)
Why Is Pubic Hair Curly? (1995)
Men in Dresses (1996)
Power over Cancer (1996)
Crossdressing (1996)
How To Get The Best Out Of Prescription Drugs (1996)
How To Get The Best Out of Alternative Medicine (1996)
How To Conquer Arthritis (1996)
High Blood Pressure (1996)
How To Stop Your Doctor Killing You (1996)
How To Overcome Toxic Stress (1996)
Fighting For Animals (1996)
Alice and Other Friends (1996)
Dr Vernon Coleman's Fast Action Health Secrets (1997)
Dr Vernon Coleman's Definitive Guide to Vitamins
    and Minerals (1997)
Spiritpower (1997)
Other People's Problems (1998)

novels
The Village Cricket Tour (1990)
The Bilbury Chronicles (1992)
Bilbury Grange (1993)
Mrs Caldicot's Cabbage War (1993)
The Man Who Inherited a Golf Course (1993)
Bilbury Revels (1994)
Deadline (1994)
Bilbury Country (1996)

short stories
Bilbury Pie (1995)

on cricket
Thomas Winsden's Cricketing Almanack (1983)
Diary Of A Cricket Lover (1984)

as Edward Vernon
Practice Makes Perfect (1977)
Practise What You Preach (1978)
Getting Into Practice (1979)
Aphrodisiacs - An Owners Manual (1983)
Aphrodisiacs - An Owners Manual (Turbo Edition) (1984)
The Complete Guide To Life (1984)

as Marc Charbonnier
Tunnel (novel 1980)

with Dr Alan C Turin
No More Headaches (1981)

with Alice
Alice's Diary (1989)
Alice's Adventures (1992)

What the papers say about Vernon Coleman

- 'Vernon Coleman writes brilliant books.' THE GOOD BOOK GUIDE
- 'The revered guru of medicine.' NURSING TIMES
- 'Perhaps the best known health writer in the world today.' THE THERAPIST
- 'The Lone Ranger, Robin Hood and the Equalizer rolled into one.' EVENING TIMES
- 'Britain's leading health care campaigner.' THE SUN
- 'Britain's leading medical author.' THE DAILY STAR
- 'Brilliant.' THE PEOPLE
- 'The patient's champion.' BIRMINGHAM POST
- 'The medical expert you can't ignore.' SUNDAY INDEPENDENT
- 'Dr Coleman writes with more sense than bias.' DAILY EXPRESS
- 'Outspoken and alert observer.' SUNDAY EXPRESS
- 'All commonsense and no nonsense.' HEALTH SERVICES MANAGEMENT
- 'Vernon Coleman is the people's doctor.' DEVON LIFE
- 'The doctor who dares to speak his mind.' OXFORD MAIL
- 'Refreshingly sensible.' SPECTATOR
- 'He writes lucidly and wittily.' GOOD HOUSEKEEPING
- 'The doctor with the common touch.' BIRMINGHAM POST
- 'Clear and helpful.' THE GUARDIAN
- 'His message is important.' THE ECONOMIST
- 'It's impossible not to be impressed' WESTERN DAILY PRESS
- 'Refreshingly forthright.' LIVERPOOL DAILY POST
- 'His advice is practical and readable.' THE NORTHERN ECHO
- 'His advice is optimistic and enthusiastic.' BRITISH MEDICAL JOURNAL
- 'Dr Coleman speaks openly and reassuringly.' OXFORD TIMES
- 'One of Britain's leading experts.' SLIMMER MAGAZINE
- 'Acknowledged authority.' THE OBSERVER
- 'Dr Coleman manages to present complex technical arguments in a simple and understandable way... he argues very cogently and convincingly...what he says is valid and needs to be said.' NURSING TIMES
- 'A godsend.' DAILY TELEGRAPH
- 'The layman's champion.' EVENING HERALD
- 'One of the country's top health experts.' WOMAN'S JOURNAL

How To Publish Your Own Book

Vernon Coleman

BLUE BOOKS

Contents List

PREFACE

ACKNOWLEDGEMENTS

PART 1: PERSONAL EXPERIENCE 15

PART 2: WHY YOU SHOULD PUBLISH YOUR OWN BOOK 32

1. Your book gets published *32*
2. Your book is published the way you wrote it *35*
3. You don't have to worry about what is fashionable *35*
4. You can publish your book quickly *36*
5. You get to control the way your book looks *37*
6. You control marketing and advertising *37*
7. You can make more money by publishing your own books *39*
8. Publishing your own books can give you independence *42*
9. When you publish your own book you get to know what is happening straight away *45*
10. You don't have to deal with a conventional publisher *45*

PART 3: WRITING YOUR BOOK: PUTTING IDEAS DOWN ON PAPER 48

1. Writing non fiction *48*
2. Writing fiction *49*
3. Do you need an editor? *52*

PART 4: TURNING YOUR WORDS INTO A BOOK: HOW TO BE A PUBLISHER 54

1. Work from home *54*
2. Get to know your basic costs *55*
3. Getting your book printed *57*
4. Hardback or paperback? *58*
5. Choosing a title *60*
6. Cover design *64*
7. How many should you print? *67*
8. How much should you charge for your book? *71*
9. Register your copyright *74*

PART 5: HOW TO SELL YOUR BOOK 75

1. Bookshops *75*
2. Mail order *78*
3. Direct Mail *81*
4. Direct selling finances *82*
5. You must have confidence in what you are selling *86*
6. Selling non fiction *87*
7. Selling fiction *90*
8. Promoting your book *91*
9. Advertising you can get for free *93*
10. Advertising you have to pay for *96*
11. Loose inserts *111*
12. Record the responses to your advertisements *112*
13. Laws, regulations and regulators *114*
14. Reviews *121*
15. The importance of the free gift *124*
16. No risk ordering – the importance of the guarantee *124*
17. Returns are a selling opportunity *127*
18. Despatching your books *128*
19. Buying your stationery *129*
20. Insurance *129*
21. Ordering reprints *129*
22. Sales representatives *129*
23. Staff *131*
24. Should you charge for postage and packing? *131*
25. You need an address where orders can be sent *132*
26. Handling telephone calls *132*
27. Taking credit card orders *133*
28. Dealing with queries *133*
29. Packing books *135*
30. Processing orders *136*
31. Keeping track of where the orders have come from *137*
32. Keeping the accounts *138*
33. Customer care *138*
34. Develop your backlist *140*
35. Selling a book is the beginning – not the end *141*

PART 6: INCREASE YOUR PROFITS 142

1. Serial rights *142*
2. Foreign rights *144*
3. Multimedia *145*
4. Selling names and addresses *151*
5. Start a newsletter *151*
6. Export sales *155*
7. Publish other people's books *156*
8. Never stop watching and learning *156*
9. Always try to make your business grow *158*
10. Public lending right *159*
11. Promotional gifts *159*

Glossary Of Publishing Terms 160

Preface

The purpose of this book is simple. I intend to show you how to turn ideas into books and books into money.

This is a warts and all view of self publishing. I have not disguised or hidden any of the hazards or dangers. There are many problems to overcome if you intend to publish your own book, and if you try self publishing in a half-hearted sort of way you will almost certainly end up frustrated, disappointed and with a financial loss. You will also have a bedroom and garage full of cardboard boxes stuffed with books for many years to come.

On the other hand if you decide that you really want to publish your own book and succeed (both in selling lots of books *and* making money) then I hope that this book will help you by explaining what, in my experience, you should and should not do. This book explains and explores the dangers and the pitfalls as well as the many advantages. If you don't know where the hazards lie how can you possibly avoid them? Naturally, I can only offer general advice. You should consult professionals for the specific help you will need. I have tried to make sure that all the information in this book is accurate but prices, specifications, regulations and so on do change often so you will need constantly to check before you rush into any commitments.

The one thing I can tell you with certainty is that self publishing can be a great deal of fun and can be extremely profitable.

(It can sometimes be a pain too. But is there any way to have lots of fun and make money without ever having to put up with a few pains?)

Vernon Coleman, Devon 1998

Acknowledgements

I would like to thank Sue Ward, John Fryer, Jean Woolley, Faye Stockwell at Publishing House; Gill Redfearn; Vicky Alhadeff; Jon Carpenter; Ernie, Rob and Jo of Arrowsmith (our book printers); Brian Stockwell of Printers; the scores of people who have helped stuff leaflets into envelopes, sort the mail and put books into bags; Maureen, Claire and Melissa of Computer Education Ltd (suppliers of our marketing software); Alan Grundy, Jane Bennett and Darren Grundy of MediAbility and David Rae (our media buyers); and our many agents around the world who have sold our books to foreign publishers.

And I would also like to thank the thousands of readers whose loyal support has helped me prove that self publishing is both possible and practical.

Dedicated to: Sue Ward and the staff of Publishing House

PART ONE
PERSONAL EXPERIENCE

"Carry on being uncommercial. There's a lot of money in it."
JEROME KERN

Back in the early 1970s I first toyed with publishing when I produced a new version of the Victorian classic *Language of Flowers*. It sold, I seem to remember, for 15 shillings or 75 pence a copy. This tiny volume received a good deal of publicity, sold out, reprinted and sold out again. I didn't get rich. But I didn't lose money.

After *The Language of Flowers* I gave up publishing. For a few years after leaving medical school I was rather busy running a general practice, looking after several thousand patients and filling in forms to keep several hundred bureaucrats happy.

After I retired from general practice to concentrate on writing books, I wrote several dozen novels and non-fiction books for large, traditional London publishers. I was represented by a literary agent working at one the smartest and most fashionable London agencies and the idea of publishing my own books never crossed my mind.

It was my cat Alice who was responsible for my first real excursion into the world of publishing.

Alice first came into my life in 1983 and we got on well right from the start (the story of my relationship with Alice is told in my book *Alice and Other Friends*).

After a few years I felt I knew her well enough to write a book with her. And so together we produced *Alice's Diary – the memoirs of a cat*. At the time it was unusual for me to write a book without having previously found a publisher. My agent usually arranged a contract before I started to write. But this book was different: I felt I had to write it, but since I wasn't quite sure how it was going to turn out I didn't think there was much point in trying to find a publisher to commission the book.

When I'd finished the book I felt it needed illustrating. I knew exactly what sort of drawings I wanted but I didn't know an illustrator I could trust to draw Alice and Thomasina (Alice's half-sister). So I did the drawings myself.

When the book was finished the typescript started a long and fruitless journey around London. Publisher after publisher turned it down.

" This isn't the sort of book Vernon usually writes" "Is it intended for children or adults?" "Who is going to buy it?" "I don't understand it" and (my favourite) "Vernon doesn't write cat books" were just some of the comments which were received from the publishing professionals.

After a year or two it was clear that no one in London wanted to publish *Alice's Diary*.

However, I felt certain that there was a market.

And so Sue Ward (who now manages the blossoming empire at Publishing House, and who is most of the rest of the 'we' in this book) and I published it ourselves in 1989. That was our very first venture into self-publishing.

At this point I would point out that the single most important piece of advice I would give to any author contemplating publishing his or her own books is to try and find someone to work with. James Joyce had Sylvia Beach of Shakespeare and Co. to publish his books. I have Sue Ward to help me publish mine and I am happy to admit that without her my publishing venture probably would not have been possible; it certainly would have not been anywhere near as successful as it is. And it definitely would have not been as much fun. Every author needs a Sylvia Beach or a Sue Ward.

I take the ultimate responsibility for the books I write and publish. I do not have a limited company (there doesn't seem any point) and I run everything out of my ordinary bank account. But Sue runs the publishing venture on a day to day basis. She edits the books I write (and I trust her judgement far more than I have ever trusted any other editor). She looks after the offices and the rest of the staff, supervises the production and placing of advertisements and liaises with printers, stationery suppliers, bankers and foreign agencies.

***

Because we were still influenced by the comments made by full time 'professional' publishers in London (the ones who were confused by the fact that a doctor who wrote straight medical books and novels had co-written a diary with a cat) I deliberately didn't put my name on the cover of *Alice's Diary*. Indeed, after the book was published we did everything we could to maintain the fiction that Alice was the sole author of the book.

When readers wrote or telephoned and asked for the name of the author we told them that the author was Alice and that she was a cat. They always seemed perfectly happy with this information. When bookshop staff telephoned to ask us who the author was (as they did with remarkable frequency) we gave them the same answer. "Really?" they would say. "How amazing." No one ever said they didn't believe us, or laughed at our claim that we lived with a cat capable of writing her own book.

Within a very short time we had sold over 10,000 hardback copies of *Alice's Diary* – large enough sales to have put the book into the bestseller lists for many weeks if we had been a 'proper' publishing company.

(Just before Christmas a hardback fiction title will probably have to sell several thousand copies a week in order to obtain a place in the Top Ten. But at other times in the year sales of a couple of hundred a week may be enough to win a place in the same bestseller list. By contrast, paperback fiction sales reach a peak in the summer. All this suggests that most hardback fiction is bought to be given as presents, whereas paperback fiction is usually bought by the would-be reader him or herself.)

The initial price of *Alice's Diary* was, I think, £6.95 though we have had to put up the price a little since those early days in order to cope with rising print, binding and paper costs (it now costs £9.95).

Despite the stern and pessimistic misgivings of the publishers in London there clearly were people who wanted to read a book written by a cat. At the time I remember being rather pleasantly surprised that we were right and they were all wrong.

These days I expect the 'professionals' to be completely out of touch with what the reading public really wants. I would be rather worried if I thought I had written a book which every London publisher wanted to put on his or her list.

When readers started buying additional copies for friends (I remember that quite early on one reader ordered eleven copies to give away as presents) and Alice started to receive fan mail we felt that our publishing adventure had started with a success.

* * *

The next book we published was *Toxic Stress*.

I had never had much difficulty in selling medical book ideas to publishers but somehow I knew that this book would never make an orthodox publisher sit up and take notice. I didn't even offer the typescript to any ordinary publishers. The success of *Alice's Diary* had given me confidence and I had discovered that I much enjoyed having total control of the publication process. *Toxic Stress*, first published in hardback, sold out and reprinted within a relatively short time. I had, very quickly, found that without people in suits in the way publishing can be a real joy.

The Village Cricket Tour – a novel describing the adventures of a cricket team on tour around the west country – came next. I can't remember why I decided to write that book. It probably just happened. I always have several dozen book ideas jostling for attention and this one just managed to clamber to the front of my brain and demand to be written next.

I remember that the initial print run was 5,000 copies and early on in the book's history most of these were stored in a barn which they shared as a home with two large, old Bentleys, our other book stock and an extended family of mice.

I also remember Sue's father looking at the rather frightening piles of books and asking me if I thought I might have printed too many.

It wasn't long before readers of *Alice's Diary* wanted to know if Alice was going to write another book. And so, in 1992, the same year as *The Village Cricket Tour* was published, along came the sequel, entitled *Alice's Adventures*.

By 1993 our fiction publishing venture was well under way.

***

At the same time as Sue and I were developing our early fiction list I was continuing to work on non-fiction books for orthodox publishers, though I was beginning to feel that self publishing might offer me a more satisfying future.

In 1994 I wrote a book entitled *Betrayal of Trust* – a book which I regarded as one of the most important books I had ever written. *Betrayal of Trust* was an extended version of a special report called *Why Doctors Do More Harm Than Good* which I had originally written for a non-profit making, campaigning magazine I published called the *European Medical Journal*.

Why Doctors Do More Harm Than Good was originally published in booklet form in 1993. It had been reprinted several times, had sold several thousand copies and had attracted a considerable amount of media attention. In one three day period alone I remember doing around twenty local radio interviews.

But the press reviewers all ignored *Why Doctors Do More Harm Than Good* because it was a small, cheap booklet.

And so during 1993 and 1994 I worked on a considerably extended version of the book to be called *Betrayal of Trust*. I wanted some review coverage because I felt that the message contained in the book was an extremely important one. I felt that *Betrayal of Trust* had two themes. I regarded it primarily as an attack on the medical profession and the pharmaceutical industry (and the dependence of the former on the latter) but also as an animal rights book since it contained the names of dozens of drugs which are sold to doctors to prescribe for patients but which are known to cause extremely serious problems (such as cancer) when given to animals. I felt then (and still believe) that the book provided the evidence which proved once and for all that animal experiments are of no scientific value, and made it crystal clear that drug companies use animal experiments despite knowing this.

I sent *Betrayal of Trust* to just about every publisher I could think of. No one was prepared to publish it. Some said the style was too 'popular'. Other publishers used the excuse that the book was too 'academic'. I rather suspected that no one wanted to publish the book because they were frightened that it might annoy the medical and scientific establishment too much.

So, with the success of *Alice's Diary* and the other self publishing ventures behind me, I decided to publish *Betrayal of Trust* myself. I didn't care whether or not it made money. I didn't even mind if it lost money. I just felt that the message it contained was so important that the book had to be published. The commercial and financial success of *Alice's Diary* made it much easier to take this decision. If I hadn't published *Alice's Diary* I doubt if *Betrayal of Trust* would ever have been published.

I had published *Alice's Diary* and the other fiction books under the Chilton Designs imprint (a name which I 'borrowed' from a former family business) but although I had published *Toxic Stress* under this imprint I didn't feel that *Betrayal of Trust* would fit comfortably alongside the growing collection of novels – which by now, also included the first of a series of novels about a fictitious Devon village called Bilbury.

The quarterly journal I had founded a year or two earlier, which had spawned *Why Doctors Do More Harm Than Good*, and which was circulating throughout the world in both English and German, was called the *European Medical Journal* and so I decided to publish *Betrayal of Trust* as a *European Medical Journal* book.

Because Sue Ward was busy running the fiction side of my book publishing programme (from a spare bedroom and garage) I published *Betrayal of Trust* with the help of a publisher called Jon Carpenter who runs his own list and helps small publishers and authors convert their ideas and typescripts and computer disks into saleable books.

Gill Redfearn, who now runs Plan 2000 (the anti-vivisection organisation which I founded) was brilliant; she helped enormously by storing copies of my early books, dealing with the cheques, posting books out to customers and generally taking charge of most of the administrative work.

Betrayal of Trust has so far been reprinted three times and there are now around six thousand copies in print. The book hasn't made any money and hasn't covered the initial research costs, but I intend to keep it in print for as long as I possibly can.

Early on I approached a solicitor and asked him to try to arrange for the *European Medical Journal* and the associated book publishing operation to be turned into a proper charity. I even planned to donate all my other book royalties to the charity in order to give it a constant income.

To my disappointment I discovered that I could not turn EMJ Books into a charity. The main problem, I understand, was the fact that the publishing programme was regarded as having 'campaigning' overtones.

The fact that I couldn't run the EMJ publishing operation as a charity resulted in my decision to bring the EMJ books within my general publishing activities and to manage them alongside the Chilton Designs fiction.

The first commercially successful book which I published under the EMJ imprint was *Food for Thought*, a book which had originally been commissioned as an international co-edition by a large publisher.

The publishers and I disagreed about the content of *Food for Thought*. They felt that the book was too controversial, too opinionated and contained too much of an attack on meat. They wanted me to remove the section on Mad Cow Disease which they did not regard as necessary. (The book was written in 1993 when it was not fashionable to regard Mad Cow Disease as a serious health problem). They wanted me to change the text. I disagreed with them and wanted to keep the book as it was. In the end I asked them if I could keep the book and abandon the contract. They agreed.

Since then *Food for Thought* has, despite being a campaigning book, proved to be a huge commercial success. It reprinted five times in the first twelve months and was our first official 'bestseller'. It was the original financial backbone of the EMJ Books imprint.

***

Every time I speak to anyone in publishing (or, indeed, to a journalist) about what I do I get the clear impression that they regard self publishing as in some way not very nice.

"So," said one journalist in the midst of an interview, "let me get this straight. You write whatever you want to write and although you pay people to read and check what you have written no one can tell you that you have to make cuts you don't want to make. You then publish what you write. And you make enough money doing this to remain independent?"

I agreed that her summary was accurate enough.

You might have thought that as a national newspaper journalist, working long hard hours for a pittance, she might have been troubled by envy. You might have imagined that she would have wanted to know how she too could do the same thing. Not a bit of it. She looked at me rather pityingly, and curled her lip. "Isn't that rather self-indulgent?" she said, cheap pen poised over her cheap notebook.

***

One of the main reasons why so many people in the publishing trade (and just how making and selling books which have been created and written by other people can be regarded as a profession rather than a trade is beyond me – although that is exactly what many publishers think) look down their fine noses at self publishing is because they regard it as a form of 'vanity publishing'.

The fact is that vanity publishing is entirely different to self publishing. In vanity publishing an author hands over money – an average of around £7,000, though the cost can be as much as £15,000 – for a publisher to produce, market and distribute his book. The publisher may have a large number of books printed but, knowing that relatively few books are likely to be sold, may only have a few hundred books bound. Most of these books will be sent to the author to give away or sell to friends. The publisher has no real incentive to sell the book since he has been paid up front. It is, incidentally, not unknown for 'proper' publishers to be involved in varieties of 'vanity publishing'.

To the pretentious, pseudo-intellectual, party-going literary set which vibrates between Bloomsbury and Sloane Square, and which regards itself as having sole rights to the production of literary work of intellectual and historic value, there are no two words quite as insulting as 'vanity publishing'. (They have to regard their work as having intellectual and historic value because, since no one wants to read it, it has no commercial value. They support their shallow pretensions by giving themselves an endless number of literary awards, grants and prizes with which to subsidise their unwanted work.)

'Vanity publishing' is sneered at because the clear implication is that the author who has paid for the publication of his or her own book has been unable to find a 'proper' publisher because no one thinks that the book is worth publishing.

There is, of course, an enormous difference between vanity publishing (a relatively passive process) and self publishing (an enthusiastically active process). The author published by a vanity publisher just wants to see his book in print. The author publishing his own book as a commercial project wants to see his book published but he is also determined to make sure that it is read by as many people as possible. The self publishing author is simply cutting out the parasitic and unnecessary middleman.

The sneerers are probably far too ignorant to know that history is littered with examples of authors who have, for many different reasons, published books which they have written themselves and which have subsequently become bestselling classics. Beatrix Potter, Walter Scott, J.M. Barrie, Lewis Carroll, Walt Whitman, T.S.Elliot, Virginia Woolf, D. H. Lawrence and Mark Twain are just a few of the well known self publishing authors who spring to mind. Other modern self publishing authors include Anaïs Nin and Frank Harris.

And the sneerers are too out of touch to realise that so called 'literary' publishing (the sort which is supported with the aid of public grants, commercial prizes, sponsors and other artificial financial support) is much, much closer to vanity publishing than self publishing. The term vanity publishing could be more accurately applied to many of those who sneer most venomously at self publishing.

Many of the big publishing houses make so many losses that it is difficult to avoid the feeling that they are now the true 'vanity' publishers of our time. They often publish badly-written, unimaginative books which no one wants to read and which certainly do not make money. When a publishing house fails to sell enough books to make a profit (as many do these days) and is then supported by some other division of the conglomerate which owns the publishing house, it is difficult to see why that isn't a variety of vanity publishing – with the editors as well as the authors being supported by some commercial sugar daddy.

By contrast, author/publishers who take responsibility for the whole process can publish what they write without interference, can keep control and can, if they work at it, make a living out of what they do.

I am, I confess, puzzled by the widely held notion that there is something rather odd or distasteful about an author publishing his own work. When a singer or group sets up their own record label they are widely thought of as clever to look after themselves (and keep out of the clutches of the big companies). When a writer does the same thing it often seems to be regarded as improper.

Indeed, I am convinced that the author/publisher will, in the future, become a figure in the same mould as the actor/manager of the theatre of a few decades ago, and the actor/director in the modern cinema.

***

"Why on earth are you planning to give away all your secrets?" asked an astonished friend when I told him that I was planning to write this book.

I didn't even have to think before giving him the answer.

The simple fact is that I love books. I love writing them. I love reading them. I love collecting them. Books are, for me, the most effective way for anyone to communicate with, and establish a rapport with, any number of total strangers. A good book can take me to another place where I can forget this sometimes awful world. A good book can entertain me, inform me, amaze me and educate me. I can read a book at my own pace. I can read it indoors, outdoors or in the bath. I can put it down, leave it and go back to it when I'm ready. I can write my own notes in the margins.

I am constantly surrounded by books and I never leave the house without at least one stuffed into my bag or my pocket. All my jackets have pockets which have been stretched by having books pushed into them. I would no more dream of boarding a train or an aeroplane without two or three books than I would dream of travelling without my shoes.

I always take a book with me when I visit the dentist, go to the doctor or have a luncheon appointment. (You never know, the person with whom you are supposed to be having lunch might be late – giving you the opportunity to read a few more pages.)

But the failure of most people working in the publishing industry to understand just how special books really are has worried me for some time.

Under the smiling but malignant influence of the elegantly-suited men and women of the marketing department (who are so ignorant, so utterly out of touch and so unsympathetic towards books that many regard television, hand-held games and computers as competition!) most publishing companies are these days devoting their resources exclusively to the publishing of books which fit neatly into pre-ordained categories.

The usual publishing practice is for men and women in suits to decide what they think people want to read – and to then commission writers to give them what they think people want.

One publisher has a success with a book on embroidery, written for left-handed blind people. A second publisher then says "we must have one of those too" and so an editor is instructed to commission a book on embroidery, written for left-handed blind people. However, by the time this book comes out the market is saturated and the book is a disaster and ends up on the remainder shelves.

Meanwhile, if an author is reckless enough to suggest writing a book on embroidery for right-handed deaf people the editors will throw up their hands in horror and say "we've never done anything like that, we're not sure it will work".

If the 'suits' happen to have decided that books on hang-gliding are likely to be all the rage next year then your series of illustrated essays on the joys of hang-gliding will probably find an enthusiastic publisher who will happily hand you a fat cheque.

But if you want to write a book on bungee jumping when the 'suits' have decided that the market for such volumes has plunged downwards out of sight then you will be unlucky and your book will remain unpublished.

Publishing today is in a mess because publishers don't understand books, authors or readers. Most publishers insist on publishing what they *think* people want to read. They commission authors to write books for which they *think* there is a market. To a decerebrate publisher this may seem like a good idea – but it isn't.

I'm a writer. I want to write what I want to write. I don't want to have to worry about whether a book is going to sell (or how I am going to sell it) until I have written it.

(I don't really want to have to worry about how to sell my books at all. But until publishers show some slight sign of intelligence I will continue to publish my books myself.)

Most people who work for large publishing companies today seem to have little or no real love for books. They don't understand books and they certainly don't understand authors. Many give the impression of not even liking authors very much. (I know one publishing company which prefers authors not to set foot in its elegant headquarters.)

Modern publishing is very much a trade – and, I am sad to say, a distinctly low grade one at that. People who work in publishing are, sadly, too often patronising, impertinent and woefully ignorant about the business they are in.

People who work in publishing have always been poorly paid. In the old days people who loved books went into publishing simply because they loved books (and they enjoyed meeting and working with authors). They didn't mind the low pay and the terrible, often archaic, working conditions.

Today things are rather different: big company book publishing is still poorly paid but it now simply attracts not very bright, third-rate people who don't have the talent or the intelligence to get jobs working for tabloid newspapers or TV production companies.

***

Because their authors are unknown (and do not, therefore, have an established army of book buying fans) first novels are regarded by most publishers as unpublishable. Publishers prefer to give vast sums of money to established hot-shot bestselling authors, to celebrities (who may not be able to write but whose fame or notoriety is regarded as a short cut to the bookseller's till and, ultimately, to the book buyer's pocket) and to eminent politicians, generals and captains of industry (who may not be able to write either but whose reputations can thrill the impressionable publishing company executive who wants to be able to tell his golfing chums that he has just come from a meeting with the President, the Prime Minister or the General.)

Naturally, bestselling authors, celebrities and top politicians all expect to be given large advances (which will quite probably never be earned back) and a good deal of editorial and other in-house support.

Not surprisingly, this all means that many new authors simply cannot get their books published. There simply isn't any money left over for publishing a thousand copies of a book by an unknown author which might, or might not, prove to be commercially successful, and which might, or might not turn, out to be the beginning of a lengthy and profitable career.

A few years ago the publishing industry was composed of a vast variety of firms: some small and friendly, often owned and run by a single entrepreneur or by a family, and some huge and impersonal with affiliated companies all over the globe. This variety ensured that the unknown author did stand a chance of getting a book published. A small company might be run by someone with more passion, might be less constrained by the rigours of the marketing department and the demands of the accounts department and might be more prepared to risk some money on a publishing venture which might, or might not, pay off. If the venture did pay off then the small publisher would hope to recoup his investment either by publishing subsequent books or by selling paperback, book club and other rights to larger publishing houses. It was, for example, quite common for a small publisher to produce hardback editions of numerous new novels and non fiction books by new authors and to recoup some of the costs (and possibly make a profit) by selling book club rights and paperback rights in one or more of the selected books.

But, as a result of an apparently endless series of takeovers, the publishing industry has changed dramatically in the last few years.

***

Since I first started writing books (around a quarter of a century ago) I have published dozens of books with many of the biggest, most successful and best known hardback and paperback publishing houses in the United Kingdom.

I was able to earn a living writing books. I had books on the official bestseller lists. And I could, I suppose, have carried on for the rest of my life in much the same way.

But to be absolutely honest I never had as much fun writing books for 'proper' publishers as I have in the years I have been writing and publishing my own books.

When I used to write for big publishers just about every book I ever published involved a battle.

It took years to find someone brave enough to publish *Bodypower*. Publisher after publisher insisted that there was no market for such a book. And yet *Bodypower* went straight into the *Sunday Times* Top Ten and the *Bookseller* bestseller lists and has never been out of print since. It has been translated into over a dozen languages and extracts from it have appeared in scores of newspapers and magazines around the world. I have made several television series and a radio series based on it.

When the original paperback version of *Bodypower* went out of print a mass-market paperback house bought the rights. Their edition went out of print before it was even published. I took the rights back and sold the book to another publisher. When they, in turn, remaindered their version I bought up all their stock (around 2,000 copies), gave them away and published my own edition.

The publisher who had remaindered the book had been selling it at a low price and in pitifully small quantities. In the first eighteen months after we took back the rights to *Bodypower* we had 10,000 copies of our paperback £9.95 edition in print (most of them sold).

I could fill a book with stories like this. For example, my book *People Watching* was turned down by many publishers, but our paperback version sells for £9.95 and we have so far sold over 12,000 copies in the UK. The book has also been sold in the US and numerous foreign language rights have also been sold. Yesterday I heard that a Chinese publisher has bought the rights to publish *People Watching*.

I have very little respect for modern editors and publishers. They live in an enclosed world in London and seem to me to have very little idea of what the world wants to read. Literary editors are, it seems to me, even worse! Both varieties are, largely, failed writers; men and women who are important now and who make the most of their borrowed power because they know that they are destined to be forgotten. Because they feel frustrated at their own lack of writing success they delight in putting down the real writers with whom they come into daily contact.

***

It isn't difficult to see why many major publishing houses are currently either making losses or such small profits that their owners and shareholders are desperate to get out of the book publishing business.

The biggest and most important problem is that many publishers have totally lost touch with their market. Publishing houses have become so large and impersonal that they no longer have any instinct for what book readers (the customers who ultimately pay the food bills for authors, editors, printers and booksellers) are likely to want to buy.

The trouble began a decade or two ago when judgements about which books to commission (and ultimately publish) were taken out of the hands of editors (who, despite their knowledge, experience and track record were regarded, as a species, as being far too 'artistic' and 'unbusinesslike' to be allowed to take such important decisions) and given to smart-suited, cool-headed men and women who were specialists in the field of 'marketing' and who would, it was claimed, be able to use modern scientific methods to forecast in advance the sort of books which should be published.

This was a big mistake.

I have no reason to doubt the claim that marketing experts can forecast, prejudge and even manipulate our tastes in a wide range of commodities from clothes to food and from cars to furniture but forecasting, pre-judging and manipulating tastes in the entertainment business is a notoriously difficult exercise and book publishing is, I suspect, uniquely difficult even within the entertainment industry.

(When I classify books as being part of the entertainment industry I am not confining myself to fiction. Many types of non fiction book are also, primarily, bought and read as 'entertainment'. In addition, it is important to remember that a high percentage of books are not bought to be read at all but to be given away as presents. Buying a present is a very different business to buying something to read but the oh-so-clever marketing people at the big publishing houses do not yet seem to have come to terms with this apparent contradiction.)

The big problem the marketing people face is that their science (for want of a better word) is largely based upon what has happened in the past. Generally speaking they are not themselves innovative or truly creative and, even more important, they are not good at comprehending the potential value of new ideas. This is not so much a consequence of their own, personal intellectual shortcomings as of the limitations of a science which is essentially historic.

How, if you base all your predictions on what has happened in the past, can you possibly make any wise judgements about a new book which does not fit into any of yesterday's categories?

Marketing people will, of course, claim that they get around this problem by performing market research to define the current tastes and desires of different groups. But again this is a nonsense. If a proposed new book contains a new untested idea how can people possibly tell you if they like it until they have had a chance to read it (or at least look at it)? Marketing research is firmly rooted in the past.

It is certainly possible to identify a general need (for example, a carefully worded research programme might identify a need for a book on diverticulosis, trainspotting in Bavaria or the history of needlework in the eighteenth century) but identifying a general need is by no means the same thing as guaranteeing a market for a particular book.

The first big problem with books (and the first reason why they are unique creations which present unique marketing problems) is that they are all different and their differences are created and defined by the idiosyncrasies, tastes, skills, frailties, egos and prejudices of their authors (and sometimes, when editorial work is unacceptably intrusive, by their editors too).

The second big problem with books (and the second reason why they are unique creations which present unique marketing problems) is that the people who read them are all different too – and all have their own very special needs, hopes, expectations, prejudices and egos. No two readers respond to a book (or an author) in exactly the same way. When someone reads a book they inevitably develop some sort of relationship with the author. And the way people interact when they meet one another varies constantly. Jack may like Jill but Dora may think Jill stinks. Dick may love Dora and Dora may love Dick but Jack and Jill may think that Dick is unbearable.

There is nothing quite so personal as the choice of a book to read (choosing a book as a gift is a very different exercise). Men and women will happily buy chairs, beds, cars, carrots, lampshades and other items from a strictly limited repertoire of opportunities. But when choosing a book they expect to be able to select from several thousand possibilities.

It is, therefore, quite impossible to say with certainty that because there is a need

---

THE RISK TAKERS

FASCINATING FACT

Books have for centuries been the most important source of vital information and independent thought. Even today many television programmes and newspaper stories which appear to break new ground are taken from books.

But as more and more publishing houses are taken over by huge international conglomerates with political agendas of their own to fulfil so it becomes less and less common to see the main, orthodox publishing houses taking on anything which may offend governments or large businesses.

Small, one man or woman, publishing houses do take more risks than the big publishing companies. But if books are to continue to be a source of vital information for the public, and a medium for original and alternative thought, then it will be through self publishing and not through publishing by corporate consensus or marketing committee.

for a book on trainspotting in Bavaria commissioning a book on trainspotting in Bavaria will result in steady and predictable sales. It may be true that there is a market for such a book but the book which is produced may not be the book that people want to buy.

Marketing people claim that they can get around this problem by talking to people and finding out what they are reading. This is nonsense. People in different areas read different books. Their future buying habits are not necessarily influenced exclusively by what they have read in the past. And people lie about what they read in exactly the same way that they lie about what how many cigarettes they smoke and how much alcohol they drink. (Ask most people what they have read recently and they will always give you the names of titles which they think will impress you – rather than the titles of the easy to read novels they have really been reading. How many people being interviewed for a job or university place will admit to reading and enjoying light fiction?)

The marketing people claim that they can influence purchasing habits by demanding the right type of cover or the most alluring title. But not even doing this will guarantee a 'bestseller'. The moment the marketing scientists think they know what colour covers are most attractive someone will break the mould and prove that public tastes have changed.

The truth is that the only way to find out for sure whether or not there is a market for a book is to publish the book and try to sell it.

All this might sound rather depressing – as though publishing must inevitably be a hit and miss affair.

But this isn't entirely true.

Nothing – cover design, price, size, paper choice, editing – is anywhere near as important as what is in the book itself. A well written book, written more out of a sense of passion than a desire to satisfy a market need, will always have a decent chance of finding a market. I would go further: a badly edited, poorly produced, overpriced book that is well written with passion will, in the long term, always sell better than a well edited, well produced, cheap book that is poorly written and which has been composed without passion. Most important of all, a well written book which has been written by an author prepared to put his or her passion on the page is the only sort of book that will acquire that one quality which establishes a book as a success: word of mouth recommendation.

Since I started publishing my own books I have followed one simple rule (actually, it is the same rule that I followed when I wrote books for other people to publish): I only write books that I want to write and that I can feel passionate about. I then put a little bit of my soul into the book. An author should bleed onto the page when he is writing, for it is only through his blood that the book can come to life.

Only then, when I have written a book, do I worry about the format I will choose (should it be a hardback, a paperback, a booklet, an audio tape or a mixture of all those things) and about how I am going to find people to read it.

***

Thanks to Alice and her two books I am convinced that self publishing is now the purest form of publishing available to an author. I believe that in future, the large publishing houses which traditionally and currently dominate the literary world will simply produce the books which the marketing men believe will sell in the largest quantities.

In the future real books – written from the heart, with passion and with no thought of commercial purpose – will have no place in the large publishing house. Only authors who are prepared to publish their own work will see truly original, creative, uncommissioned work in print. Around the world today the best, most original and most exciting books are being published either by authors themselves or by small publishing houses run by authors and their friends.

Self publishing is, it seems to me, the main hope for the future of books and the future of publishing. Self publishing is probably the only way that controversial, troublesome, dangerous books are now likely to be published. Big publishing houses don't like to publish books which they think might attract lawsuits or bad publicity. Big publishing houses tend to be owned by international media tycoons who are too well aware of the commercial danger of annoying governments, lobbyists, big companies and pressure groups. A publishing company which is part of a conglomerate with complex trans-border interests has to be careful not to publish anything which might prove embarrassing or commercially damaging to another part of the empire.

***

The great beauty of having my own publishing imprints is that I can write the books I want to write – and then worry later about how to sell them.

Many of the books I have chosen to write would not have been published by a modern publishing conglomerate. And yet most of the books I have chosen to write and publish have been reprinted (some of them many times) and have sold well. Many of our books would have been on the bestseller lists if we had sold more through the bookshops (where the official bestseller lists are created) and less through the post direct to readers.

I run my publishing imprints rather in the way that I believe old fashioned publishers used to operate. I write books which I want to write (rather than books which I know will be commercially successful). And at the end of the financial year I hope that the books which sell well will have earned enough to subsidise the books for which there has not been such a clear market.

You may have different motives. You may be wealthy enough to subsidise your publishing operation without making a profit. You may, on the other hand, want every book you publish to make a profit.

So far I have published around forty of my own books – in a very short space of time. I have found it far more enjoyable than writing books for traditional publishing companies. I can write exactly what I want to write with no interference. I use the profits I make from the current books to pay for new books.

Having my own publishing imprints means that I can publish the books I want to

SO YOUR BOOK HAS BEEN REJECTED?

FASCINATING FACT

The fact that a publisher rejects your book doesn't mean that the book is no good – or unpublishable. It could just as easily mean that the publisher has returned your book without even looking at it (let alone reading it). Or it might mean that the publisher is an utter moron who would find earning a living sticking tickets onto parked cars an intellectual challenge. George Bernard Shaw reported that he had sent his first book to "every publisher on the English speaking earth I had ever heard of". The book was rejected by them all. Thomas Pirsig's classic 1970s bestseller *Zen and the Art of Motorcycle Maintenance* was rejected by 121 publishers.

Many famous authors whose books went on to become major bestsellers published their books themselves in order to get them in print and noticed. Beatrix Potter published *The Tale of Peter Rabbit* herself and when *The Rubaiyat of Omar Khayyam* was rejected the translator published it himself.

Below there is a list of just a few of the many great books which were rejected when first submitted to publishers. Some of these books were rejected not once, not twice but dozens, scores and in some cases more than a hundred times.

The Ability To Kill ERIC AMBLER
Northanger Abbey JANE AUSTEN
Molloy SAMUEL BECKETT
The Old Wives' Tale ARNOLD BENNET
The Bridge over the River Kwai PIERRE BOULLE
Naked Lunch WILLIAM BURROUGHS
The Postman Always Rings Twice JAMES M CAIN
The Mysterious Affair at Styles AGATHA CHRISTIE
Claudine in School COLETTE
The Rock Pool CYRIL CONNOLLY
Freye of the Seven Isles JOSEPH CONRAD
The Ipcress File LEN DEIGHTON
The Ginger Man J.P. DONLEAVY
A Study in Scarlet ARTHUR CONAN DOYLE
This Side of Paradise F. SCOTT FITZGERALD
Madame Bovary GUSTAVE FLAUBERT

.... continued overleaf

The Diary of Anne Frank ANNE FRANK
Lord of the Flies WILLIAM GOLDING
The Wind in the Willows KENNETH GRAHAME
The Tin Drum GUNTER GRASS
A Time To Kill JOHN GRISHAM
Tess of the D'Urbervilles THOMAS HARDY
My Life and Loves FRANK HARRIS
Catch 22 JOSEPH HELLER
The Torrents of Spring ERNEST HEMINGWAY
Kon Tiki THOR HEYERDAHL
Ulysses JAMES JOYCE
Lady Chatterley's Lover D.H. LAWRENCE
The Spy Who Came In From The Cold JOHN LE CARRÉ
The Law of Life JACK LONDON
Gentlemen Prefer Blondes ANITA LOOS
Man Meets Dog KONRAD LORENZ
The Naked and the Dead NORMAN MAILER
The Razor's Edge W. SOMERSET MAUGHAM
Moby Dick HERMAN MELVILLE
Peyton Place GRACE METALIOUS
Tropic of Cancer HENRY MILLER
Lolita VLADIMIR NABOKOV
Animal Farm GEORGE ORWELL
A Dance to the Music of Time ANTHONY POWELL
Remembrance of Things Past MARCEL PROUST
Man and Superman GEORGE BERNARD SHAW
The Jungle UPTON SINCLAIR
The New Men C.P. SNOW
Tristram Shandy LAURENCE STERNE
Lust for Life IRVING STONE
Walden HENRY DAVID THOREAU
Barchester Towers ANTHONY TROLLOPE
The Time Machine H.G. WELLS
The Book of Merlyn T.H. WHITE
Lady Windermere's Fan OSCAR WILDE
Poems WILLIAM BUTLER YEATS
War and Peace LEO TOLSTOY

Other authors whose work was rejected include: Charles Dickens, Graham Greene, Alexander Dumas, James Thurber, William Faulkner, Erle Stanley Gardner, Paul Gallico, Robert Graves, Zane Grey, John Irving, Henry James, P.G. Wodehouse, Rudyard Kipling, John Knowles, William Saroyan, Dr Seuss, Neil Simon, Gertrude Stein, Walt Whitman and Thomas Wolfe.

write, quickly and without any outside interference. A traditional publisher will usually take between 12 and 24 months to turn a manuscript into a published book. Books which are likely to annoy the establishment or attract legal opposition often remain unpublished.

Of course, there are some snags with self publishing. Writing and publishing your own book takes more time than just writing it. You will be completely responsible for any libel problems or other legal trouble. (These days you will probably be responsible anyway). There will be no one to hold your hand, give you advice, congratulate you and take you out to lunch on publication day. You will be on your own (without someone to pat your hand and tell you not to take any notice) if you get bad reviews.

You will probably find that publishing your own book will take over your whole life (not to mention your home for the books have to be stored somewhere).

You will be sneered at by oh-so-superior literary editors, bookshop managers and, probably, even other authors. Your books will not appear on the bestseller lists (however many copies you sell) and you may not win any awards, accolades or prizes because there will be no one to propose you for any. (Though you can always put yourself forward for a prize.) You will also have to learn a lot of new skills.

Publishers like to make everyone think that there is some mystery about what they do. There isn't. The difficult thing about publishing is writing the book. And publishers don't do that. If you are intelligent enough to write a book then you are certainly intelligent enough to publish it. Self publishing is fun. It is something you can do with pride. And it is also something that you can do with profit. The self publishing author can become independent and free of traditional publishing constraints. The self publishing author can, by making his books profitable, free himself to write the books he wants to write. And that has to be good for authors, readers and society in general.

PART TWO
WHY YOU SHOULD PUBLISH
YOUR OWN BOOK

"As repressed sadists are supposed to become policemen or butchers so those with irrational fear of life become publishers."
CYRIL CONNOLLY

"All that is necessary in the production of a book is an author and a bookseller, without any intermediate parasite."
GEORGE BERNARD SHAW

1. YOUR BOOK GETS PUBLISHED

This may sound a little obvious but with more and more books being published every year, and just about every literate and semi-literate individual in the western world apparently determined to prove the truth in the old adage that everyone has at least one book in him or her, the competition is fiercer than ever before.

"It is a truth universally acknowledged that 99% of the population of the United Kingdom are determined to write a book and get it published," wrote Christopher Sinclair-Stevenson in *The Times*.

Getting a book published the traditional route is not easy. If you don't have a good contact within a publishing house or don't have an agent (don't think that finding an agent is an easy way to get published because it isn't – it can be just as difficult to find an agent for a book as it can be to find a publisher) the chances of your finding a publisher prepared to accept you as an author are, to put it mildly, not terribly good.

Even authors with a strong track record, whose previous books have sold well, may find it difficult to find a new publisher if their old editor retires or moves to another company.

Just about every country in the world is now publishing more books than ever before but, paradoxically, if you think that this means that more authors are getting their books published then you are probably wrong. A rapidly rising percentage of books are international co-editions. An American author will write a book for an American company which will then sell that book to publishing houses all around the world. The book will be designed in such a way that the overall format remains stable, as do the illustrations, while the text is translated and slotted into the available spaces. The rise in the popularity of international co-editions does not mean that a few authors are getting extremely rich on foreign royalties because the publishers of international co-editions are usually pretty mean with the royalty rates they offer. And, sadly, it is not at all unknown for authors to receive a modest flat fee for a book which subsequently sells hundreds of thousands of copies in scores of countries around the world.

These days there is absolutely no guarantee that you will find a publisher even if you produce a masterpiece. In fact your chances of finding a publisher for a masterpiece, or for anything that might be considered 'original', will be slimmer than ever.

The problem today is that medium and large-sized publishing houses are almost completely controlled by the men in suits. The money men decide which books will be bought and published and the editors in a publishing house simply buy and edit what they are told to buy and edit.

Managing editors and editorial directors all like to pretend that they have the same degree of power as their predecessors had a few decades ago but although they may be able to fool themselves they don't fool anyone else.

Because the men and women in suits (the marketing men) don't understand books at all (and don't have much sympathy with authors – whom they generally regard as something of a nuisance) they tend to shy away from anything unusual. As far as they are concerned all books should fit into nice, neat categories and if a book can't be fitted into a nice, neat category then they won't have anything to do with it.

If your book can't be quickly slotted into a well defined genre such as Romantic Fiction, Gay Issues, Science Fiction, Mechanical Engineering or European Travel then the people in the publishing house simply won't know what to do with you or your book. Write a romantic book about a gay couple who travel through Europe repairing trains and no one in modern publishing will know how to categorise what you've written.

Because they have no real feel for the business they are in, and have virtually no imagination at all, the men and women in suits are always looking for books that are rather like the books that they think are currently popular. So, if there is a book about flower arranging on the bestseller lists then all the men and women in suits will be demanding more books on flower arranging. If a biography of a dead, homosexual film star seems to be popular the men and women in suits will be screaming for biographies of dead, homosexual film stars.

Sadly, there are several flaws with this sort of technique. The first is that bestseller lists are virtually irrelevant these days and their only really practical purpose is to make editors and authors feel good. The fact that a book is on the bestseller lists does not, paradoxically, mean that it is particularly popular or that it is selling a lot of copies.

The second flaw is derived from the fact that large modern publishing houses are a little like large modern tankers: they don't move very quickly. Tanker captains have to plan a long time ahead if they want to turn left or right (or even port or starboard) because their vessels are so vast that they do not respond very quickly. Publishing houses, for no good reason at all that I am aware of, are equally cumbersome. There is usually a year's gap between the moment that a man in a smart suit notices that a book on embroidery seems to be popular and the moment that his publishing house brings out its own 'cloned' book on embroidery. By that time, of course, the demand for books on embroidery will be even smaller than it was when the man in the suit thought it was at its peak. It is this which explains why so many books produced by large publishing houses go straight from the printers to the remainder shelves in bookshops everywhere.

In order to prove how incompetent publishers are, frustrated authors will occasionally copy out an existing masterpiece and submit it to various publishing houses. Six months later they announce, with great glee, that editors at forty top publishing houses have all rejected James Joyce's *Ulysses*, Ernest Hemingway's *A Moveable Feast*, Shakespeare's *Hamlet* or some other classic.

This should not, I fear, surprise anyone.

The first reason that this happens is that books which are not commissioned are often rejected automatically and virtually unread. A junior editor or the tea lady may glance over the manuscripts which pour in through the mail but most will be kept for a couple of weeks (in order to ensure that the author believes that their baby has been given careful consideration) and returned (as long as the author enclosed the requisite number of stamps, of course). Unless the junior editor or the tea lady has a passing acquaintanceship with the world's classics there is little chance that a genuine masterpiece will receive more attention than three hundred pages copied out of the local telephone directory.

The second reason why even masterpieces are rejected by modern publishing houses is that even if (by some stroke of astonishing good fortune) a senior editor happens to take a peek at a book which falls out of a brown paper parcel the chances are that the senior editor will know very little, if anything, about books or literature and would not recognise James Joyce, Ernest Hemingway or William Shakespeare if they wandered into the building and asked for an appointment.

You might, quite wrongly, gather from all this that I have a rather jaundiced view of modern publishers. You might feel that I have a chip on my shoulder and that I am merely grinding an axe about publishers because I can't get my own books published and have to publish them myself.

Nothing could be further from the truth. Since I began publishing my own books I have turned down offers from many 'orthodox' publishers so that I can carry on publishing my own books.

I give thanks every day for the fact that the posh publishers no longer understand books or publishing. I am delighted that they don't understand what readers want and even if they did they wouldn't know how to give it to them.

I earn my living as a writer and I have, during the last few years, taken back the rights to most of my books because I think I can publish them more successfully than anyone else. I happily and enthusiastically sell my books to foreign publishers but I publish the original editions of my books myself and I haven't offered a book to a British publisher for many years.

2. YOUR BOOK IS PUBLISHED THE WAY YOU WROTE IT (WITHOUT A KID FRESH OUT OF COLLEGE TELLING YOU WHAT TO WRITE OR HOW TO WRITE IT)

When I first started writing books, what now seems like a century and a half ago, the editors I met seemed to be keen to help me make my book better. They suggested changes and improvements but it was up to me to decide whether or not to accept the changes.

By the time I gave up writing books for big publishers I was fed up of editors telling me what to write – and how to write it.

I remember that the comments I received from an editor who was supposed to be working with me on a book I was writing about food were, for me, the last straw.

As I mentioned earlier I had included a section detailing the hazards of eating meat. The editor told me that I had to amend my comments about meat because if I left them in we would lose readers. I protested, arguing that I could not possibly put something with which I disagreed into a book I was writing.

In my view she seemed to regard the book as a commodity rather than something I was creating out of my beliefs, my passion and my knowledge. In the end we had a huge row and I took the book away from the publisher for whom she was working. I later published the same book that she had refused to accept and called it *Food for Thought*. The book has been hugely successful and well received by reviewers and (far more important) by readers.

3. YOU DON'T HAVE TO WORRY ABOUT WHAT IS FASHIONABLE (AND SO YOU CAN PUBLISH WHATEVER YOU LIKE)

Most authors write books because they enjoy writing. Many also write because they have something they desperately want to say.

There are, of course, exceptions to this rule.

Someone I know who earns a living in the media told me one day that he thought he should write A Book. He was aware that I had at that time written quite a number of books and as he looked at me a thought bubble appeared above his head. "I think it is about time I wrote A Book!" he said, delighted with what was for him I suspect a uniquely original and neurone-bruising notion.

It seemed to me to be clear that although he didn't have any burning desire to write a book, nor any great passion which he felt could be best expressed in book form, he felt that writing a book would be a good career move. Sadly, many books which are written these days begin their lives in such an unpromising way. A celebrity announces to the publishing world (through his agent) that he is ready to write a book. And a couple of marketing men in smart, expensive suits come up with an idea that is probably about as original as the wheel and as nourishing as a slice of white bread.

Until I met that celebrity who seemed to me to regard the writing of a book as a necessary step on his career path, I had never thought of books in such a way. It had never before occurred to me that anyone would simply think of writing A Book rather than writing a very specific book. I don't know whether the media personality ever produced A Book but if he did I doubt if it had any heart or soul. And I doubt if many people really wanted to read it. It is my belief that before you start writing a book it must be something that you want to write, need to write and have to write. If you don't want to write it, need to write it and have to write it then there isn't much of a chance that anyone is going to want to read it, need to read it or have to read it.

Sadly, however, many of today's publishers don't seem to have much sympathy for my rather old-fashioned attitude. They, like the media celebrity I've just quoted, regard books as marketable commodities. They happily publish books which enable them to exploit television fame and transient fashion.

Look at the new books on the bookshop shelves these days and you will see that many of them seem to have been published with the idea of cashing in on some new fashion or trend. Often it is the author him or herself who is the fashionable item around which the book has been built.

"Matt E. Mulchen is very popular with 17-19 year olds," the marketing man in a suit will tell the editors. "Sign him up to write a book."

No one gives a damn that Matt E. Mulchen is illiterate. The publishing house will hire a ghost writer to help him put something down on paper. And to be honest no one really cares whether or not the contents of the book are any good. They know that the only thing that really matters is that the cover includes a big picture of Matt.

Of course, Matt will probably be forgotten within a year or so and his book will be forgotten too. But that doesn't worry the marketing men in suits. They don't have much interest in backlist titles. They are only interested in finding a book to accompany the latest fashion and make a quick profit.

4. YOU CAN PUBLISH YOUR BOOK QUICKLY

Very, very occasionally you will read about a publisher bringing a book out in a matter of days. The chances are that the book is being published quickly in order to cash in on a crisis, a disaster or a sudden news event. A biography may be produced to tie in with a celebrity's death. A book may be produced to tie in with a famous rescue or some heroic endeavour that has gained a good deal of publicity around the world.

But these are exceptions.

Despite all the modern technology that is now available publishers seem to be taking longer and longer to turn manuscripts into books. It is commonplace for a publisher to take a year to turn an accepted manuscript into a book and not at all uncommon for publishers to take two years to go through the relatively simple process of publication.

I have no idea why the gestation period within commercial publishing houses has grown so long though my guess is that it is a result of a growth in the amount of administration. Publishing companies are now very largely run by bureaucrats who, like all bureaucrats, do not like taking any responsibility or any decisions. The result is that everything has to be done by committee. And so everything takes for ever.

If you publish your own book you will be able to turn a finished manuscript into a completed, bound book within two months without too much effort. It may take a little longer than this if the printer you want to use is particularly busy. Or it may not take that long if you happen to find a printer who has men and machinery sitting idle waiting to print your book.

The speed with which a book can be published is important to me. Sue and the staff at Publishing House once turned a computer file into a book in just five weeks. During that five weeks the book was edited, the cover was designed and printed, the book was designed, printed and bound and the finished copies were delivered to the Publishing House warehouse.

5. YOU GET TO CONTROL THE WAY YOUR BOOK LOOKS

Some publishers will show authors proposed cover art work. And some will even discuss the style their book will take. But very few publishers will talk about the type of paper that will be used. And hardly any will discuss the typeface in which the book will be printed.

Most publishers are even reluctant to divulge details of the number of books they intend to print (known as the 'print run'). Some seem to think they are divulging a State secret if they tell an author whether his book is to be published in a hardback or a paperback edition.

If you publish your own book you get to control everything. You can decide on the type of paper to be used. You decide exactly what your book looks like. You can choose the type of cover you have. Everything is your decision and your responsibility. And it is you who will decide how many copies of your book should be printed.

6. YOU CONTROL MARKETING AND ADVERTISING

It is traditional for authors to fret about the way that their book is promoted and marketed. Visit one of the large, smart bookshops in the centre of London on almost any day of the week, take a book off a shelf and pretend to examine it. Now look around and watch carefully and you will see a constant stream of slightly shabby, furtive looking individuals moving books about. They will take a book from a shelf, where it has been displayed spine out, and then put it back on the shelf so that it is displayed full face. They will take a book from a shelf and place it in a prominent position on a display table. They will move books which are well displayed into far less favourable positions. These shabby individuals are all authors rearranging the bookshop stock so that their book has a better chance of catching a potential customer's eye – and so that their rivals' books are less prominently displayed. It is, of course, a sad and entirely pointless business because within seconds of their leaving the shop their book will have been moved aside by some other author eager to ensure that his volume is well displayed.

"There weren't any books in the shops" is one of the most popular complaints made by authors. But it is by no means the only complaint. Other popular cries are: "There weren't any reviews", "There wasn't any advertising" and "They didn't fix up any interviews".

No one who writes a book and has it published by an established publishing

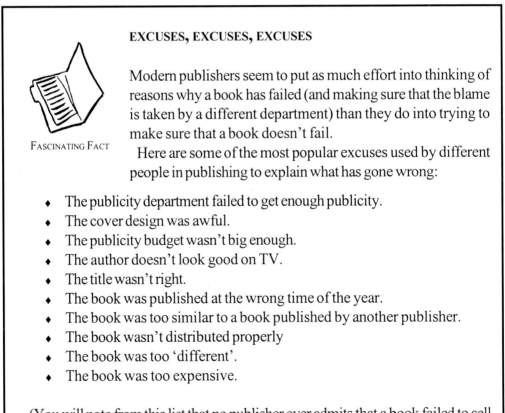

EXCUSES, EXCUSES, EXCUSES

Modern publishers seem to put as much effort into thinking of reasons why a book has failed (and making sure that the blame is taken by a different department) than they do into trying to make sure that a book doesn't fail.

FASCINATING FACT

Here are some of the most popular excuses used by different people in publishing to explain what has gone wrong:

- The publicity department failed to get enough publicity.
- The cover design was awful.
- The publicity budget wasn't big enough.
- The author doesn't look good on TV.
- The title wasn't right.
- The book was published at the wrong time of the year.
- The book was too similar to a book published by another publisher.
- The book wasn't distributed properly
- The book was too 'different'.
- The book was too expensive.

(You will note from this list that no publisher ever admits that a book failed to sell because they produced a rotten book that no one wanted to buy.)

house is entitled to call himself a real author until he has made at least two of these complaints.

(Most authors will not, of course, moan to their publisher. Authors tend to be timid people, overawed by publishers and constantly worried that if they make too much trouble their next book will not be accepted. The author will usually keep his complaints to himself, store them up inside him in a deep dark place and perhaps share them occasionally with his partner, his closest friends or his analyst.)

If you publish your own book then you are in charge. You can buy as much advertising for your book as you can afford. You can do promotional posters, leaflets, bookmarks, window stickers, beer-mats and T shirts. You can, if you wish, advertise your book on the sides of buses, on huge poster sites, on television, on radio and in the cinema.

The failure to market, advertise and distribute copies of a book may sometimes seem to an author to be a sort of censorship. By taking control of all this an author can discover just whether or not his book is truly being suppressed. (Or whether the public just don't want to buy it.)

The downside to all this upside is, of course, the fact that if your book does not sell well you have no one to blame but yourself. The author who publishes his own book is denied access to most of the traditional excuses for failure. If your book isn't well displayed in your local bookshop there is no editor to ring with a heartfelt complaint. If your self published book is not advertised in the national press you have only yourself to blame. If your book isn't promoted on television then there is no one to take the blame but you. If your book doesn't get reviewed in the national press there is no one to ring but yourself.

7. YOU CAN MAKE MORE MONEY BY PUBLISHING YOUR OWN BOOKS

Sadly, most published authors earn such a pittance from their work that they have to do something else to earn a living. For every author who receives a million dollar advance there are thousands of authors who, after they have deducted their essential expenses, receive an hourly rate that would draw a derisory sneer from a fast food outlet employee.

But if you publish your own book there is a good chance that you will not only be able to make a living out of doing something that you enjoy but that you will be able to build up and develop a small but profitable business.

Publish your own book and you may become independent and in control of your own life and destiny. You will acquire new skills and as the months and years go by you will become increasingly confident about your ability to publish as well as write. It is, incidentally, perfectly possible to make money out of selling fiction as well as non fiction.

Publishing your own book does require a modest initial capital outlay (although, since printers commonly give 60 days' credit it is, if you have strong nerves, perfectly possible to get your book printed and then rely on selling enough copies to pay the printer). But once you have learned some of the basic facts about self publishing there is no reason at all why you shouldn't make a profit.

I have seen it said that anyone contemplating self publishing should only ever self publish a book which they think they could sell to a traditional publisher. Forget that advice. It was undoubtedly well meant and I can understand why it was said but it probably originated with someone who had no experience of modern publishers. The first book which I published was *Alice's Diary*. I published it myself because my agent

FINANCIAL TIP

A HIGHER PRICE MEANS BIGGER PROFITS

As a self publishing author you may not sell as many copies as you might if your book was published by an orthodox, traditional publisher. But you can nevertheless make more money. Publishers tend to sell their books far too cheaply – and give authors a very small percentage of the profits.

So, for example, consider my non-existent friend Jack Middleton who is writing a book called *Dine from your Garden* in which he explains how he and his family grow all the fruit and vegetables they need simply by planning carefully and rotating crops in a small suburban garden.

If Jack's book is published by Bigthick Books they may (if they are extremely successful) sell 3,000 copies of a paperback edition which they sell at £3.95. Of the £11,850 that the book brings in Jack will probably receive 7.5% or £888.75. If Jack has received an advance for his book the advance will have to be paid off before he receives any royalties. In contrast the retail bookshops and wholesale outlets will receive about half the total sum received – or £6,000. The rest of the income produced by the book will be swallowed up in paying the publishing company's fixed costs and providing it with a small profit. On a book like this there will be probably be virtually no money at all spent on publicity and advertising.

If, on the other hand, Jack decides to print 1,000 copies of his book and sell the books himself at £9.95 he will only need to make 10% profit on the sales in order to make more money. If he sells some of his books direct (without going through bookshops) he will save the 50% that bookshops and wholesalers take. And by publishing himself he will save the money the publisher has to pay in salaries, expenses, rates, rent and so on.

Self published books tend to sell in smaller quantities. But the profit potential is usually much higher.

could not find a publisher prepared to take it. When the book had sold 20,000 copies in hardback I felt that I was justified in thinking that my judgement about the book had been fulfilled. My guess is that over half the books I have published myself would have been rejected by commercial publishers.

Not all the books I write make money. But this doesn't worry me at all. Having published around forty of my own books I run my publishing operation like an old-fashioned publisher. I use the books which do make money to subsidise the books which don't make money.

Sometimes, when I finish writing a book I know very well that the book will never make a profit. I know too that no commercial publishing house would even consider the book. As my own publisher I don't have to worry about things like that.

When I had finished writing *Fighting for Animals* I knew that it would never make a profit. When I had finished writing *Betrayal of Trust* I made a deliberate decision that the book would never be allowed to make a profit. Every time the book goes into profit I spend the profit on buying yet another advertisement.

I never expected my books *Men in Dresses* or *Crossdressing* to make a profit. I published them because I thought that the message they contained was worth the cost of publication.

But, on the other hand, when I published *Alice's Adventures* I was pretty confident that it would make a profit since its predecessor *Alice's Diary* had done so well.

Sometimes a book will turn out to be more or less commercially successful than expected.

When I had finished writing *The Man Who Inherited A Golf Course* I wasn't really sure that it would make a profit. But I had enjoyed writing the book and I thought it was worth publishing. It was first published in 1993 and in its first few years of life it was reprinted several times and sold over 8,000 copies in hardback at £12.95. Moreover the book continues to sell steadily and consistently. A TV company and a film production company are now both interested in turning the book into a film. The book has turned out to be successful and profitable and an important title on our fiction backlist.

On the other hand when I published the second edition of *Know Your Drugs* I expected the book to be a steady seller and quite profitable. So far it has proved difficult to sell and it has lost money. This is almost certainly because I published the book in an expensive, hardback format.

Sue Ward and I wanted to experiment a little and produce a book that looked really good and felt good to handle. But the unit cost was so high that it has been impossible to make the publication of this volume profitable. We will probably have to reduce the price dramatically in order to move the remaining volumes. The downside is that there won't be much of a profit. The upside is that there won't be much of a loss either – and we have learned a valuable lesson.

I believe that there are only three reasons to do anything: to try to change the world, to have fun and to make money. Sometimes it is possible to do things which satisfy all these three objectives. More often the success of one objective means that one is more capable of pursuing another objective. (So, for example, making money doing something which is dull may enable you to enjoy an experience which is fun.) Only very occasionally is it really possible to combine all three of these reasons.

The books which best satisfy all three objectives are the two books I wrote with Alice. Both *Alice's Diary* and *Alice's Adventures* were fun to write and illustrate. Both have made money and helped to subsidise the research and production of other books. And both may, I hope, help change the world a little by encouraging people to think more about animals as thinking, sensitive creatures instead of as objects.

8. PUBLISHING YOUR OWN BOOKS CAN GIVE YOU INDEPENDENCE

Your happiness on this earth depends to a very large extent upon the amount of freedom you have. It is difficult to find contentment if you are a slave. And, in our society, the amount of freedom you enjoy depends to a certain extent upon the amount of money you have because money can buy you freedom.

I do not approve of this state of affairs. It is quite wrong. But it is how things are and it would be foolish to deny it or to try to fight against it.

Clearly, therefore, making money – on your own terms – is an integral part of finding contentment. You have to turn the skills you didn't know you had into cash.

Your first step on the road towards making money should be to analyse and make an inventory of your assets. What are your special and most significant assets? Do you have knowledge to sell? Can you entertain, amuse, inform or educate? You must know all the advantages that you have to offer. You must know how you can benefit others and there must be a measurable and profitable result which you can define, promote and sell.

Unfortunately, most authors cannot make a living out of their writing. The vast majority of authors who have had a book published by a conventional publisher have to do something else to earn a living. By the time bookshops and publishers have taken their cut there is very little left for the author. The traditional author's hardback contract gives an author 10% of the published price but this percentage is often reduced (in some cases considerably) if the edition is a paperback or a low-cost book club edition. In comparison the bookshop and the wholesaler (whose sole task is to act as intermediary between the publisher and the reader) will often take half (or even more) of the published price. If you think that the bookseller's role is worth five times the role of the author then you will undoubtedly regard this as an entirely equitable state of affairs.

Publishing and selling his own book gives the author a chance to take control of his own destiny. Any author who has confidence in the value of his own work ought to publish himself or herself at least once.

If you find the financial implications of self publishing rather frightening then I suggest that you consider these facts (which may help soothe your worries a little).

The first important thing you should remember is that all investment is gambling. If you have savings which you give to your bank to invest on your behalf then you are, whether you like the idea or not, gambling. You are gambling that the bank will not go broke. And you are gambling that the investment will gain value – rather than lose value. In some circumstances the risk may be slight. But it is foolish to pretend that there is no risk. And when you invest in someone else's business (as you do when you buy shares in a public company) you are handing over all management responsibility to a group of people you don't know and will probably never meet. If you invest in a unit trust or an investment trust then you are spreading your risk by putting your money into numerous companies but there is still an element of risk involved. On this occasion you are trusting the investment managers who decide which companies should benefit from your savings. If the investment manager is blessed with a brain the size of a dried pea your investment is likely to shrink rather than grow. If you decide that all this is too risky for you and you put your money in a sock and hide it under the bed then you are gambling that inflation will not eat into your savings. You will almost certainly lose this gamble and when you take the sock out from under the bed your savings will have a much smaller buying value than they had when you put the sock under the bed.

You should remember all this when trying to decide whether or not to risk investing a little money in the publishing of your own book. When you publish your own book you are backing your own skills. You are in a strong position to decide whether or not

---

FINANCIAL TIP

FOREIGN RIGHTS MEANS FOREIGN MONEY!

One of the big advantages of publishing your own book is that you get to control all the rights. Selling rights is one of the most important ways for a publisher to make money and a normal contract for a book gives the publisher an indecently high proportion of the money to be made in this way. Keep your own rights and over the years that come you should be able to acquire an albeit unsteady income from the sale of such wonders as Russian paperback rights, Korean rights, Hebrew rights, Swedish bookclub rights and South African magazine rights.

When I first had the idea of writing my book *Know Yourself* many people in publishing thought it was a daft idea (although to be fair the book was first published in the UK by Penguin). I now have the rights back and the book is published as a European Medical Journal book. The book is currently in print (and earning money) in the following foreign countries: Korea, China, Japan, Russia, Portugal, Holland, Norway, Italy, Germany and the US.

your publishing venture will be a success. There are, of course, numerous outside factors over which you may have little or no control but, generally speaking, if you decide to publish your own book you will have far more control over the outcome than you will if you give your money to someone else to manage for you.

The second vital factor to remember is that when you publish your own book you can usually delay the moment when you have to find real money until after you have received the finished books and begun to sell them. Since it is usually also possible to purchase advertisements on credit you may be able to publish your own book without any capital at all.

Having said this I must point out that personally, I wouldn't like to do this, and I would strongly recommend that you have all the money you are prepared to invest sitting in an interest earning deposit account at the bank before you start publishing. However, the 60 days that you are likely to be able to wait before you pay the printer, and the 30 days that you may be able to wait before you pay for your advertising, does give you a little extra room for manoeuvre.

The one time when you may find the credit periods of real value is when you publish your second book and find your publishing empire beginning to blossom. If your first book is just beginning to become profitable, and you have established advertisements which work but you have had to spend all your available money on a reprint or on new equipment, then you may be able to use these periods to help with your cash flow.

The third factor which you should remember (and which may help to influence your decision about whether or not to go it alone and publish your own book) is that if you publish your book with the genuine intention to make money out of the venture, then you will hopefully be allowed to offset the costs of your venture against any other income you have when you have to declare your earnings to the tax man. Printing costs, postage, advertising costs, stationery costs and so on should all be deductible. If you have to go to Italy for two months to do research for a book then the costs should be deductible. You will, of course, have to keep a full record of your outgoings and your earnings but it is always nice to know that the Chancellor of the Exchequer (who will eventually share in your good fortune if your book makes a profit) will share the risk with you as well.

Fourth, it is worth remembering that the government wants you to spend your money on frippery so that you remain a wage slave. Governments like people who spend all their money on things they don't really need for it is people who spend who help to keep the economy strong and if people only spent their money on essentials most folk wouldn't need to work more than a few hours a week. If your income and outgoings are balanced rather tightly and you feel nervous about publishing your own book then perhaps it might be worth taking a look at your outgoings to see whether or not you can cut anything from your weekly and monthly budgets. Publishing your own book might enable you to gain personal and financial independence for the first time in your life. You may feel such a goal makes a few short term sacrifices worthwhile.

9. WHEN YOU PUBLISH YOUR OWN BOOK YOU GET TO KNOW WHAT IS HAPPENING STRAIGHT AWAY

A friend of mine who is an extremely successful author is always moaning that his publisher will never tell him how many copies his latest book is selling. He is a rather paranoid individual, prone to conspiracy theories, and he always believes that his publisher is keeping something from him. (He is, therefore, a fairly normal author.)

The fact is, however, that publishers never like telling authors how their books are doing. I don't know why this is but sales figures are treated as Top Secret Information in most commercial publishing houses.

When you publish your own book you can get all the information you want just as quickly as you want it. I receive a faxed printout from Publishing House every day. This tells me exactly how many books have been sold that day – and whether the books were sold through bookshops or through mail order advertisements. I receive a stock list once a week which tells me how many books are still in stock. This enables me to order reprints (hopefully) well in advance of their being needed.

10. YOU DON'T HAVE TO DEAL WITH A CONVENTIONAL PUBLISHER

In the good old days authors and publishers were very much on the same side. They worked together to make sure that every book had the best possible start in life. The publisher was the commercial midwife who helped turn the author's vision into practical reality. Authors trusted publishers to be fair with them and to offer them a decent contract. Publishers had faith in their authors and enjoyed working with them.

Things have changed.

"The sense that the publisher and the writer are no longer on the same side, and that the agenda is driven by accountants and lawyers who will never even look at the work in question, makes authors suspicious," wrote Kate Pool in *The Bookseller* in 1997. "Authors fear that contracts are one-sided and sometimes obscure or even misleading."

"Feeling the pinch from wholesalers and retailers, and competition from other conglomerates," she wrote, "publishers in turn seem to be trying to make up the difference by squeezing their authors, rather than attempting to address the roots of their problems."

In the 'old days' publishers often had a stake in the publishing company for which they worked. Many publishing houses were relatively small and privately owned. Editors would have a real say in the company and would feel secure in their working environment.

Sadly, these days many editors spend much of their time watching their backs and worrying so much about their own financial futures that they cannot afford to show exceptional loyalty to their authors.

"Editors – and by editors I mean those self-effacing creatures who actually believe they are there to help the author rather than their own image, and who might even work on the script to make it better or more saleable – are in short supply. Big publishing companies, once spurred on by editors, and then fuelled by accountants, now tend to be motivated by marketing persons," wrote Christopher Sinclair-Stevenson in *The Times*. "This is a mysterious breed, much influenced by the size of advance which the author has been paid and not prepared to waste valuable time in building up the career of a writer over a series of books."

In the worlds of technical and academic publishing royalties and advances are often small and sometimes non-existent. Authors are often encouraged or even coerced into handing over their copyright – simply in order to see the book in print.

In trade publishing (where books are aimed at the general book-buying public) publishers have introduced many complications to the traditional author contract. Half a century ago it was commonplace for authors to receive 15% to 20% of the published price of a book. Today a figure of 10% for hardbacks and 7.5% for paperbacks is much more usual.

Contracts may include a clause that allows for higher royalty rates when book sales reach a certain level. But there is some suspicion among many authors about the ability of computerised accounting packages to take full account of these contractual niceties.

Royalty rates are often extremely low on books sold to book clubs and may reach zero when books are sold to magazines to be given away as a 'free' offer. (The excuse here is that the book is being given away as a promotion though it is sometimes difficult to see what is being promoted in those circumstances and how much benefit there can possibly be for the author.)

More and more publishers are offering authors 10% of subsidiary rights which used to remain with the author in their entirety. Receipts from paperback rights, serial rights and foreign rights are divided up so that the lion's share of the money goes to the publisher rather than (as used to be the case) the author. The 80:20 split often used to mean 80% to the author and 20% to the publisher. These days it is likely to mean 80% to the publisher and 20% to the author.

And these days it is not unknown for a publisher to put the royalties from a book that sells well against the unearned advance for another book by the same author. This sort of thing never used to happen but is now apparently considered 'fair dealing' in the new publishing world.

The author who publishes his own book, and then sells off rights himself to magazines, newspapers, foreign publishers and so on, may find that he is not only freed from much unnecessary frustration but also far more likely to be able to make a living from his writing.

"So, are publishers really necessary?" asked Christopher Sinclair-Stevenson. "They certainly are for a couple of dozen established writers who can command hefty advances..." he replied, answering his own question.

But "As publishing companies increasingly tend to overlook the relevance, let alone the sensitivity, of authors," he continued, "and as the degree of incompetence and lack of communication increases within these publishing companies, authors may need something very different from what they could expect in the past...If all else fails...they can publish themselves. They cannot be worse than publishers."

When I talked to one frustrated and disappointed author, suggesting that he should publish his own book he told me that if he couldn't get his book published by a 'proper' publisher then he didn't want it publishing at all.

I'm not sure how he would define a 'proper' publisher.

But in my view a 'proper' publisher is anyone who turns an original typescript (in whatever mechanical or electronic form it may be) into a saleable book – and then ensures that the book is read by as many people as possible.

48

PART THREE
WRITING YOUR BOOK: PUTTING IDEAS DOWN ON PAPER

"I suffer from the disease of writing books"
CHARLES LOUIS DE SECONDAT

Before you can write a book it is probably best to start with an idea. The quality of your book, whether it is to be a volume of fiction or non fiction, will to a very large extent depend upon the quality of your idea.

You may think that I am stating the obvious. Sadly, I am not. Not all books are born of passion. Some result from a commercial coupling between publisher and author, inspired by the computerised equivalent of the tinkle of cash registers.

1. WRITING NON FICTION

The first thing you must remember when you start writing a non fiction book is that most people buy non fiction books for one of two very simple reasons:

- they want to be entertained or
- they want information and advice

Try to decide which sort of book you want to write before you write it. This will help you write a better book.

If you decide to write a book based on your thirty years experience as a schoolteacher you will find the book easier to write if, before you start to hammer the keyboard, you know whether you intend to entertain your readers with rib tickling anecdotes from your days in the classroom (*Thirty Years Of Chalk And Duster*) or you intend to provide neophyte schoolteachers with a clear guide to the pitfalls which await them in a teaching career (*How To Be A Successful And Happy Teacher*).

I am not, of course, suggesting that these two approaches are mutually exclusive. If you are writing a practical, informative guide book you should (if you can) try to make your book as readable and as entertaining as possible. There is no reason at all why a book bought for information shouldn't be fun to read. And the corollary is true too. If you are writing an autobiography there is no reason why your book should not be full of titbits of useful information.

But unless you have some idea of the sort of book you plan to write when you sit down and start writing the chances are that it will lack any sort of framework and, more important, a clear purpose.

I have been shown numerous typescripts put together by would-be authors. The commonest problem I found was that although many of them were the right length to be books, they simply *weren't* books. There was nothing holding all the words together. There may have been twenty chapters, sixty thousand words and a foreword. But twenty chapters, sixty thousand words and a foreword do not automatically make a book.

When writing a non fiction book you have to start with a purpose. Why do you want to write the book? Why do you have to write the book? Why is the book necessary?

When you know the answers to these simple questions you will find it relatively easy to work out what to put in the book.

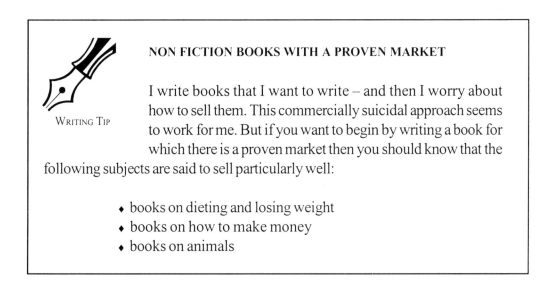

NON FICTION BOOKS WITH A PROVEN MARKET

WRITING TIP

I write books that I want to write – and then I worry about how to sell them. This commercially suicidal approach seems to work for me. But if you want to begin by writing a book for which there is a proven market then you should know that the following subjects are said to sell particularly well:

- ◆ books on dieting and losing weight
- ◆ books on how to make money
- ◆ books on animals

2. WRITING FICTION

This is primarily a book about how to publish – rather than a book about how to write. But here are a few tips which you might find useful:

- ◆ If you are trying to write a funny scene you need to move logically, step by step, so that when you reach an absurd and illogical (and hopefully funny) conclusion you will have reached it via a series of perfectly sensible and entirely logical steps. Start with a normal world and then, step by step, take your readers to a place where they never imagined they could possibly find themselves. To be funny you must move from normal to abnormal in imperceptible steps.

- ◆ Unless you are extremely experienced it is sensible to plan what you are going to write before you start. It is perfectly true that once you have developed your characters they may (if they have been properly developed) decide for themselves what happens. But this will only happen if the characters are well drawn.

♦ Before you sit down and start watching sparkling dialogue trickle out of your keyboard you need to have some sort of theme: you need a conflict. Once you have sorted out your conflict (the dramatic theme for your story) you need to decide on the characters through whose eyes the drama will unfold. When you have your conflict and your characters you can start plotting. It is only when you have conflict, characters and plot sorted out that it is worthwhile sitting down and starting your tale.

♦ If you are planning an unusual, exotic or extraordinary adventure story then make your hero a perfectly ordinary man or woman. This will automatically heighten the contrast and therefore the tension in your story.

♦ Choosing whether to write in the first or third person is probably one of the first big decisions you have to take. It is easier to get the reader immediately involved in what is happening (and to produce a sense of drama) if you use the first person because the reader is seeing everything through the narrator's eyes. The two big disadvantages with using the first person are that you can't easily describe the main character in the book and you are committed to looking at everything that happens from one point of view.

♦ Don't get bogged down in detail. You may have done six months of careful research in order to make sure that you know the background to your story. But if you are writing a novel the careful research must be invisible; there in the background but never becoming boring. If you want to show off how much research you have done then perhaps you should be writing a non fiction book.

♦ To make your characters real let them eat meals and wear clothes. Describe the meals they eat and the clothes they wear. This will enable you to tell your readers a great deal about the characters you are describing.

♦ To make your book move smoothly from one point to the next think of your book broken down into scenes in a play. Try to 'see' your book being acted out on screen or stage.

♦ Readers have to care about your characters. They have to like or love your heroes and they have to loathe and detest your villains. If readers don't care about the people in your book then you won't have a book worth reading.

♦ Don't put too many of your own views into a novel. Let your characters put forward your views in their words, deeds and actions. Great novelists eliminate themselves from their work but create characters and plots which burn with life and sear themselves into the mind of the reader.

THE SECRETS OF SUCCESS

WRITING TIP

In 1903 legendary writer Jack London wrote an article called *Getting Into Print* in which he explained the secrets of his success. His article is still valid and contains vital truths of which all writers should be aware.

"Don't quit your job in order to write unless there is no one dependent upon you. Fiction pays best of all, and when it is of fair quality is more easily sold. A good joke will sell quicker than a good poem, and, measured in sweat and blood, will bring better remuneration. Avoid the unhappy ending, the harsh, the brutal, the tragic, the horrible – if you care to see in print the things you write. Humour is the hardest to write, easiest to sell, and best rewarded.'

'Don't write too much. Concentrate your sweat on one story, rather than dissipate over a dozen. Don't loaf and invite inspiration; light out after it with a club, and if you don't get it you will nonetheless get something that looks remarkably like it. Set yourself a 'stint', and see that you do that 'stint' each day; you will have more words to your credit at the end of the year. Study the tricks of the writers who have arrived. They have mastered the tools with which you are cutting your teeth. They are doing things, and their work bears the internal evidence of how it is done. Don't wait for some good Samaritan to tell you, but dig it out for yourself."

"See that your pores are open and your digestion is good. That is, I am confident, the most important rule of all. And keep a notebook. Travel with it, sleep with it. Slap into it every stray thought that flutters up into your brain. Cheap paper is less perishable than grey matter, and lead pencil marking endure longer than memory. And work. Spell it in capital letters, WORK. WORK all the time. Find out about this earth, this universe, this force and matter, and the spirit that glimmers up through force and matter from the maggot to the God-head. And by all this I mean WORK for a philosophy of life. It does not hurt how wrong your philosophy of life may be, so long as you have one and have it well. The three great things are: GOOD HEALTH, WORK and a PHILOSO-PHY OF LIFE. I may add, nay, must add, a fourth – SINCERITY. Without this, the other three are without avail. With it you may cleave to greatness and sit among the giants."

3. DO YOU NEED AN EDITOR?

Some critics of self publishing claim that the biggest problem faced by authors who do their own publishing is that they have to manage without a good editor.

I fear that such critics are rather out of touch since good editing hasn't been regarded as an essential part of publishing for many years.

It is, of course, perfectly true that a good editor can greatly improve the balance and accessibility of anything that has been written. But it is also true that no one ever buys a book, a newspaper or a magazine because it has been well edited.

Readers may (quite reasonably) moan if the publication is littered with misprints and painful grammatical errors but the simple fact is that editors are secondary to the whole business of writing. They are far, far less important than writers and much less important than printers. They are, in many ways, the most expendable part of the whole publishing business.

Sadly, many editors do not recognise their role in the whole hierarchical publishing system and rather give the impression that they consider themselves to be by far the most important figures in the business.

You and I know better.

A writer can write without an editor but an editor can't do anything without a writer.

When I used to publish my books through London publishing houses I had numerous rows with extremely young and inexperienced graduates who thought that because they had a degree, had been on a weekend publishing course and had a plastic plaque with 'EDITOR' stamped on it on their door or desk they automatically knew everything there was to know about books and publishing.

I lost count of the number of rows I had with snooty, half-baked decerebrates who thought that their few months experience of being patronising to other authors gave them the right to tell me what to put into my book (and what to take out).

My favourite trick with these literary incompetents (most of the ones I met seemed, sadly, to have relatively little knowledge of how to use semicolons and commas but a good many politically correct views, though it was the first of these I was looking for) was to invite them to look at the title page of the book we were discussing.

"Whose name do you see there?" I would ask, as sweetly as I could manage.

"Yours," the editor would reply, after a moment's hesitation.

"Exactly!" I would say. "This is my book we are talking about. If you want to write your own book then please feel free to do so. I promise that I will not make any attempts to tell you what you can or cannot include in it."

What you need instead of an editor is a sympathetic friend or relative who has a little spare time, and who knows a bit about spelling and grammar.

When you are writing and in full flow you can often overlook silly mistakes (like overlong sentences, missed commas and apostrophes or duplicated sections). A fresh eye should be able to spot these quickly and easily and suggest any corrections. Note the use of the word *suggest* – the final decision about what (or what not) to change stays with you.

ADVICE FROM AN EXPERT

Writing Tip

"A writer must reflect his world, interpret life, dig at the bare truth. He must have talent and conscience. If he has talent and no conscience he's a journalist and writes that kind of book. If he's neither, he's a hack. He becomes an advertising man or a press agent. A glorified pimp on the expense account. A serious writer needs a viewpoint of his own – not that of his employer. In a word – character. A rare commodity"

F Scott Fitzgerald

Part Four
Turning Your Words Into A Book Or How To Be A Publisher

"Publish and be damned!"
Duke of Wellington

1. WORK FROM HOME (AND YOU DON'T NEED TO FORM A COMPANY)

Don't, whatever you do, rush round to your nearest estate agent and buy or rent an office. To begin with you can run everything from a spare room in your house. You don't need much more equipment to be a publisher than you needed to write a book. You need a desk, a typewriter or a computer, a telephone and an almost endless supply of paper and pens.

If you rush out and buy or rent a special office you will immediately burden yourself with the businessman's curse: significant overheads.

We had published half a dozen books (including the bestsellers *Alice's Diary* and *The Village Cricket Tour*) before we invested in proper offices. Until that date everything had been run from home with between 15,000 and 20,000 hardback books stored in a barn and a garage. At busy times we would recruit everyone passing through to help open the mail and stick books in bags. Floors were left unhoovered while the woman hired to look after the house stuck stamps on envelopes and parcelled up books.

Eventually it all became too much to run from home and we set about looking for a building which we could turn into a centre for a small but rapidly blossoming empire. We were lucky to find a large disused workshop which we were able to turn into offices and a warehouse. It didn't take long to decide to call it Publishing House.

But even though my publishing imprints had acquired a proper home of their own I still didn't form a company.

My view is that becoming a company is probably quite unnecessary – unless you enjoy the extra administration and accounts associated with running a limited company.

I operate as a sole trader and there are, it seems to me, several advantages in working this way.

First, everything is kept relatively simple. At the end of each tax year I add up my gross income, take away the gross expenses and pay tax on what is left – the profit. I leave the fine points of discussion to my accountant and the man from the Inland Revenue.

Second, if you run all your writing enterprises as one you may, when you are starting out, be able to set any losses you make through setting up your business against profits from your other writing activities. For example, if you earn money writing articles for newspapers and magazines you may be able to set the costs of advertising your books against those earnings. If you set up a limited company your personal accounts and the company accounts will have to be kept apart and you will not have this flexibility.

The big advantage of operating a limited company is, of course, the fact that your own personal liabilities are limited. But in reality I'm not sure that this is much of a practical advantage. Being a limited company won't protect you if you publish something which turns out to be libellous. The person you have libelled will simply sue you as the author rather than as the publisher. You can't escape from that responsibility. And since no one is likely to give your company credit unless you provide some sort of personal guarantee or security (your house, insurance policy, or family jewels) you aren't likely to benefit all that much from having a limited company standing between you and your creditors. Besides, I wouldn't like the idea of using a limited company to help me avoid my personal debts.

If I eventually do form a company to operate Publishing House and the three imprints I run it will be because the whole thing has just got too large to run comfortably in its present simple state.

2. GET TO KNOW YOUR BASIC COSTS

If you think that getting your book printed will be your only expense then you are dangerously wrong – and heading for disaster.

But once you have a printing cost for your book then you can start working out the overall costs for the other essentials.

Publishing a book involves seven basic costs – most of which apply to self publishers:

1. The cost of printing or binding will usually be between a tenth and a fifth of the cover price. As a self publisher there is nothing you can do about this expense. If your book costs you £1 to £2 to print and bind then you should charge £9.95 when you sell it. The printing and binding price is the foundation upon which you can work out the other costs involved in publishing a book.

2. You should allow another 10% of the cover price for distribution – whether you send your books out by the lorry load to bookshops and wholesalers or whether you post off books individually in padded bags. Once again this cost will be unavoidable. You have to distribute your books if you are going to sell them.

3. If you sell your book through wholesalers and retailers then you will have to give them

between 35% and 50% of the published price. The self publishing author can cut this cost by giving a lower percentage to bookshops – which will usually order single copies as customers order the book from them. Bookshops are unlikely to order from a self publishing author in huge quantities. Ask bookshops to pay up front so that the money lost through unpaid invoices is slight.

4. A normal publisher will allow around 10% of the published cost of a book for over-heads (rent of premises, rates, salaries of staff, electricity, heating, telephone and so on). The self publishing author will probably have low costs in this area but it is important to remember that your self publishing venture will incur additional costs (and these should be recorded among your expenses when you submit a tax return).

5. It is fairly normal to allow 7.5% of the published price for marketing and advertising. The self publisher should not skimp on this area of expenditure. You will probably not have a sales force and you will not need to buy huge self-congratulatory advertise-ments in the trade press but since mail order sales will probably play a vital part in your growing business you must allow for buying advertisements in magazines and newspapers. The money saved on bookshop discounts should be allocated to the advertising budget.

6. The author of a hardback book will normally receive an average royalty of around 10% of the published price. The self publishing author doesn't need to worry about having to pay an author a huge advance. He doesn't even have to worry about having to pay any royalties. (Incidentally, it was reported recently that in 1996 one large American publisher wrote off about $35,000,000 worth of unearned advances while another wrote off close to $80,000,000 worth of unearned advances.)

7. A traditional publisher's final cost (and by far the most difficult to estimate) is the cost of returns. I will deal with returns at greater length later in this book. If a publisher ships vast quantities of a book in response to massive bookshop orders he may become too enthusiastic and reprint yet more books in the hope and expectation that the book is going to be a major bestseller. But if the bookshops return a high propor-tion of the books then the publisher is likely to be in deep, deep trouble. According to a recent issue of the *New Yorker* magazine the average independent bookstore re-turns about 20% of its books whereas chains may have returns of 30% upwards – around a third of all published adult trade hardback books are returned unsold in the US. Most of these books cannot be resold and unless they can find a home on the remainder shelves they are simply destroyed. Astonishingly high returns (in excess of 50%) are by no means unknown and in the world of paperback publishing are fairly commonplace. But as a self publisher you are unlikely to have high enough bookshop sales to have to worry much about returns.

3. GETTING YOUR BOOK PRINTED

I suggest that you do not try printing and binding your book yourself unless you are happy to confine yourself to publishing booklets, pamphlets and sweet little publications which look as though they have been put together by a couple of sixth-formers from the local school.

Every week I am sent copies of books which have been put together with the aid of a photocopier and then bound in booklet form (sometimes by a local printer but sometimes at home). I have a very strong suspicion that 99.99% of these publications are either given away to friends and relatives or stored in the garage or the loft until they go mouldy. A few may be sold at car boot sales or church bazaars but I doubt if many are sold to strangers. (You are a successful self publisher when you start selling your books to strangers.)

Booklets (held together with staples and without a proper spine) are fine if you are publishing purely for fun (or because you simply want to spread your word around a few friends) but if you are going to go to all the trouble of writing a book (as opposed to a booklet) then you should produce and print it properly.

Anything which contains more than 20,000 words really needs a proper spine – and that means a proper printer. Persuading bookshops and libraries to take copies of a self published volume is difficult enough. If you offer them something that looks like a home cooked booklet you will be making life unbelievably difficult for yourself.

DON'T FORGET

YOU NEED SPACE — PROBABLY MORE THAN YOU THINK

Publishing books requires space. You can't do it from the kitchen table. (Well, I suppose you could. But you would find it pretty tiresome if you had to move everything out of the way whenever you wanted to eat.)

Until your books arrive from the printers you will only need space for a computer, typewriter or writing pad and pen. But once the books arrive (and that is the point at which you will really feel that you are a publisher) you will need a lot of space. (A stack of just 1,000 books takes up a great deal of space. If you doubt me then I suggest that you collect together 100 books and see how much space they take up. At Publishing House we usually have between 30,000 and 40,000 books in stock at any one time.) You will need somewhere to store the books. You will need somewhere to store the padded bags in which you send out the books. You will need somewhere to write out the orders and you will need somewhere to weigh parcels and stick on stamps.

Finding a sympathetic and understanding printer who will help to demystify the production process is vital. And it isn't too difficult.

When I first started publishing my books I had no idea what happened to the words I had written in order to turn them into a book. And nor did Sue. But by being totally honest about our lack of knowledge we soon found a printing company eager to help us. We would send them an edited typescript and simply say "please make it into a good looking book using good paper" and a few weeks later a lorry would deliver the finished product.

Of course, this lack of knowledge did cause us to make some decisions which we might not make today. For example, when we published *Alice's Diary* we had no particular idea what size the book should be. So we simply found a book we liked the look of and said "make it this size". We had no idea that we had chosen a size which meant that a large amount of paper was wasted when the book was trimmed to our chosen size. This put up our costs, and if we had known more then we could have chosen a size which made better use of the paper which we were paying for. And of course we are now stuck with this more expensive format because all the film has been shot and it would cost a huge amount to change things for future print runs. (In some ways the added expense has been worth it because the unusual size makes Alice's books appear more like 'diaries' than if we had used a standard size; they look a little different and that all helps to make an impression when people open their mail order package.)

So my advice is be honest about your ignorance, find your helpful printer and ask him to explain things to you every step of the way.

4. HARDBACK OR PAPERBACK?

Logically there is no sound reason for publishing hardback books. They cost more to produce and therefore have to be sold at a higher price and yet the stuff that really matters (the words inside) could just as easily be put into a paperback. But here, as in many other areas of publishing, there are factors other than logic to be taken into consideration.

The first reason for seriously considering hardback publication is that the publishing trade itself still doesn't regard paperbacks as 'proper' books. If you think I'm exaggerating about this then look at the book review page in just about any broadsheet newspaper. You will see that most of the coverage is reserved for hardback books. Reviews of paperback books (even original paperbacks which have never appeared in hardback and which might, therefore, expect to be treated in the same way as hardbacks) are often tucked into a corner of the page. Similarly booksellers will usually reserve most, if not all, of the space in their shop windows for hardback books.

The second reason for publishing a book as a hardback is that you then have a

WHAT DOES THE PRINTER WANT TO KNOW?

with thanks to Rob Briggs, J.W. Arrowsmith Ltd., Bristol

PRODUCTION TIP

Format: Remember to use standard book sizes for economy reasons. Standard sizes are 216 x 138mm (demy) 234 x 156 (Royal) 246 x 171 (PC4) and 'A' sizes 210 x 148 (A5) and 297 x 210 (A4)

Typesetting: If the printer is typesetting your work he will need to know the typeface and sizes you wish to use along with the line length and number of lines per page. Chapter openings are usually 'dropped' so specify the drop required. Positions of page numbers are also required along with details of running headers (these will usually have the book title on the left hand running header and the chapter title on the right header). Specify if new chapters should start on a new page and also indicate the number of proofs required. Specify margins required. For economic production aim to achieve an even working i.e. multiples of 16 pages.

Printing the text: If you have supplied the text already typeset then you need to confirm the margins so that the printed matter can be positioned correctly on the page. You also need to discuss any illustrations which are to be included (line art, half tones or full colour) and where they are to be placed in the text. It is often most economic to have photographic plates grouped together within a signature.

Text paper: There is an almost endless variety of papers to choose from. Stock papers will usually offer the most economic option. You should ask your printer for details and samples.

Jackets: Specify 1, 2, 3 or 4 colour if you are supplying artwork and original pictures (transparencies). Remember to specify the lamination you require – gloss, matt or varnish.

Cover: Specify 1, 2, 3 or 4 colour if you are supplying artwork and original pictures (transparencies). Cover board is usually 240gsm and most printers will hold sample stocks. Specify either varnish or lamination.

Hardback (or cased) binding: Specify if to be sewn or unsewn, the board weight and binding material (the cloth which covers the boards). Supply details of blocking (the lettering which is imprinted onto the spine and front of the book). Then make sure the jackets are supplied to the bindery and give details of the delivery address.

Paperback binding: Specify if sewn, unsewn, saddle stitched, perfect or slotted.

If you are unsure about any technical terms then either refer to the glossary or discuss with your printer who should be able to help you.

chance of selling the paperback rights to a specialist (or even a mass market) paper-back publisher. It is, of course, well known that paperback publishers will sometimes hand over cheques for vast amounts of money for the right to publish a particular book in paperback in their chosen territory. Do not, however, get too excited by this possibil-ity. Sadly and unfairly, it is unlikely that a paperback publisher will even deign to look at a self published book (though it does happen – in some cases spectacularly).

The third and most important reason for considering hardback publication is that a large percentage of books are bought as presents and people prefer to buy hardback books as presents. When buying a present many people decide how much they are going to spend before they decide what to buy. And a hardback book not only fits into more present buying budget categories but it also looks a lot more expensive than a paperback. It is this third reason which you should consider carefully.

My advice is simple: if you are publishing a book which you suspect may be bought and given as a present (a novel, for example) then you should seriously consider hardback publication. If, however, you are publishing a book which will be bought largely or exclusively for the information it contains then you should probably prefer paperback publication.

WHAT DO YOUR CUSTOMERS REALLY WANT?

MARKETING IDEA

When trying to think of a title: try to decide what your cus-tomers really want from you; what are their particular fears and hopes; how can you help them satisfy their dreams and conquer their fears?

Remember that your customers don't want to buy a book – they want to buy a solution to a problem. If the prob-lem is the fact that they have a health worry then they want you to help them get rid of their anxiety. If they are overwhelmed with government forms then they want you to help them deal with the forms in less time. If they are bored then they want you to intrigue and entertain them. If they want to be able to embroi-der a tablecloth then they want you to show them how, quickly and easily.

There are over 7,000 books in print with the words 'How to...' in the title. Do not be afraid to use these two words if they are appropriate.

---

5. CHOOSING A TITLE

As a writer you will, of course, appreciate that words are powerful. It is always vital to pick the right words. Do you think that Moses would have been as successful if he had come down from the mountain with *Eleven Suggestions* or *Nine Hints*?

If your book is going to be successful then your title has to catch the eye and fire the potential reader's imagination. If you are selling a non fiction book then you should remember that you are selling solutions, not problems! (Most people have plenty of problems. It is solutions they want and need.) Your title will, to a large extent, be your shop window. It will appear in your catalogue and (hopefully) in other people's catalogues. It is all the browser will see when peering at a row of book spines in his local bookshop or library

So how do you choose a title?

To a large extent finding a good title is something of a knack. But it is a knack that can be acquired. The quickest and easiest way to discover which titles work best is to look around your own bookshelves (or the bookshelves in a local bookshop or library) and write down the titles which really grab you.

When you have done this write down all the benefits and advantages of your book on lots of separate pieces of paper. When you've finished look at all the words you have written down. You may see a title struggling to get out from everything you have written.

There are no hard and fast rules when it comes to selecting a title.

Sometimes a very simple, prosaic and obvious title is best. There is little point in trying to be clever, and looking for a witty double entendre, if you are planning to write (or have written) a book which offers information or advice on a specific subject. My books about specific diseases usually have very simple titles (such as *How To Conquer Arthritis*, *Relief from Irritable Bowel Syndrome* and *High Blood Pressure*). My theory is that an individual who has arthritis, and who is looking for a book on the subject, knows exactly what he or she wants. A clever title might be missed as he or she scans the shelves.

Sometimes a witty or clever title may be more appropriate. And sometimes you can produce a bestseller by thinking up an entirely new word. One of my most successful books is *Bodypower*. (I have always had to fight hard to persuade publishers and catalogue writers to print the title as one word rather than as two words). After *Bodypower* had been a success I wrote *Mindpower* and *Spiritpower* – thereby giving me a trilogy.

PRODUCTION TIP

DESIGNING YOUR BOOK COVER OR JACKET

Do remember that the cover will eventually end up wrapped around the book. Always take a mock-up or proof of the proposed cover or jacket, wrap it around a book of roughly similar size to the book that is being planned and see what it looks like.

PRODUCTION TIP

WHAT MAKES A BOOK?

First and foremost, a right hand page in a book is known as a 'recto' and the reverse of that page is known as a 'verso'. Printers will use these words endlessly and it will save confusion and embarrassment if you remember these two terms now!

A book is made up of three basic sections:

♦ **The stuff at the front:** known as prelims (short for preliminaries). These pages may numbered in two ways, either starting at page 1 and running consecutively throughout the book, or as an isolated group of pages numbered with roman numerals (with the book proper starting on page 1). Any running headers or footers should be removed from these pages.
♦ **The stuff in the middle:** your book.
♦ **The stuff at the back:** postlims or end matter consisting of the index, appendices, reference lists and your advertisements for other books. This section should always start on a new page. Any running headers or footers should be removed from these pages.

The stuff at the front may consist of any or all of the following (those items in italics must always be present in any proper book). The rest can be included or excluded as you see fit – or according to the number of pages you need to fill.

• The half title page – just the title of your book and always on a recto.
• Verso blank or used for a list of your other books (in my case, now running to 3 or 4 pages).
• *The title page* – contains the full title (including any subtitle) of the book, your name as author and the name of the publishing company (and any logo). This page is always a recto.
• *Title page verso* – contains all the data on your book. A sample of a title page verso is shown on the opposite page.
• Contents page with blank verso (unless the contents extend over the page).
• List of illustrations with blank verso (unless the list extends over the page).
• Foreword, preface or introduction with a blank verso.
• Acknowledgements.
• Verso used for any dedication.

Your book should then start on a recto

Your book can be laid out however you wish. Chapters can run on or start on a new page. We once had new chapters starting always on a new recto but this did tend to leave a lot of white space dotted through the book. If your chapters start on a new page then decide if you want them to start in a dropped position (slightly lower down the page) which is usual. Do you want a dropped capital letter at the start of the first sentence? Will you use sub headings? If so, how will they stand out from the rest of the text. Try and decide on a style sheet for the various elements of your book to keep the publication looking like a proper book.

The stuff at the back will contain any other material needed to make the book work. You may decide you need an index which can be quite a complicated task. Use other books to help you decide what to include – and remember that you must work from a final proof copy of the book when compiling your index to ensure that you get the entries and page numbers correct. There are whole books on indexing, and specialist indexers who do nothing else. If your non-fiction book is particularly complicated then you may want to consider using a professional indexer. If you have written any other books (even if they are published by someone else) consider including advertisements on the final pages.

title page verso taken from *High Blood Pressure*

Note that we have included the dedication on the title verso. This was necessary to ensure that an economic number of pages (or signatures) was used. An extra page for the dedication would have taken us over the maximum number of pages allowed for economic printing.

Published in 1996 by the European Medical Journal. Publishing House, Trinity Place, Barnstaple, Devon EX32 9HJ, England

Much of this book first appeared under the title 'Everything You Need To Know About High Blood Pressure' in the series 'Dr Vernon Coleman's Healthbooks for all the family', published by Severn House in 1985. This edition first published in the United Kingdom by European Medical Journal Books 1996.

Reprinted 1998 (twice)

The right of Vernon Coleman to be identified as the author of this work has been asserted in accordance with the Copyright, Designs and Patents Act 1988.

ISBN: 1 898947 79 1

DEDICATION
To Tom and in the memory of Alice, Dick, Harry and Timmy

A catalogue record for this book is available from the British Library.

Printed and bound by: J.W. Arrowsmith Ltd., Bristol

6. COVER DESIGNS

If you intend to sell most of your books by mail order then, in theory at least, cover design is not terribly important. By the time your readers see your book they will have already paid for it and unless your cover appears in your advertisements they will have done so without knowing what it looks like.

But, in my view, cover design does matter – however you intend to sell your books.

It matters for several important reasons.

First, although it is difficult to get bookshops to order and stock a book published

PRODUCTION TIP

JACKETS AND COVERS – SAVING WORK AND HEARTACHE

When ordering your book covers or jackets you need to know how wide the spine will be on the finished book. This may sound obvious, but it's surprising how often this can get overlooked during the production process.

You can use these simple tips to work out how wide the spine of your finished book will be:

For perfect bound or slotted paperbacks

$$\frac{\text{Volume of paper x N}^\circ \text{ of pages x grammage of paper}}{20,000} = \text{spine width}$$
(round up to nearest mm)

For perfect sewn hardbacks

$$\frac{\text{Volume of paper x N}^\circ \text{ of pages x grammage of paper}}{20,000} + \text{2mm (min)} = \text{spine width}$$

An even simpler tip – get your printer to work it out for you!

It's possible that the company which prints your covers will not be the same as the people who print your books. You can save yourself a great deal of work and heartache by getting the two companies to liaise and work together to make sure that everything goes smoothly (make sure you do this in writing and keep a copy on file). If something then goes wrong and the jacket or cover doesn't fit the book you can quite reasonably blame the two sets of professionals and let them get on with apportioning blame, sorting out who's going to pay for the mistake and then making sure that you receive books with the right covers as soon as possible.

by any small publisher it will be a great deal more difficult (and probably impossible) if the book cover is not attractive. You may find this hard to believe, and even harder to accept, but it is not at all unknown for large bookshops to decide whether or not to buy a book solely on the cover. The bookshop buyers who work this way claim that they simply don't have time to read all the books they are offered and that consequently they have to choose books according to how they look. They further excuse this seemingly barbaric policy by claiming that bookshop customers use a similar technique when deciding which book to buy.

PRODUCTION TIP

EXTRA COVERS

When you order the jackets or covers for your book you will need more than the number of books you are planning to print. You will need these extra jackets or covers for three reasons:

♦ Your book printer will need what are known as 'binders overs' (usually 10% of the print run). These are needed in case there are problems during the binding or jacketing process.

♦ You can use extra jackets or covers for publicity and promotion. The run on cost of covers is extremely small and you will obtain a good promotional aid at a very low cost.

♦ You will need extra jackets to restore damaged hardbacks for resale. Keep the jackets flat and use them to replace covers which become ripped or marked. (Hardback books which are returned by bookshops or customers will usually have a marked or ripped dust jacket)

I am afraid that to a certain extent they are right. Potential buyers certainly flick through a book, look at the contents list and (if there is one) the index, and read the first paragraph and another sentence or two taken at random somewhere in the middle of the book, but it is the cover that gets more attention than anything else. And, surprisingly perhaps, it is the back cover that gets most attention. A staggering number of publishers still produce books that have entirely blank back covers. I consider this to be extraordinarily inept; it is akin to committing professional and commercial suicide. It is mostly hard cover publishers who produce books with nothing on the back but some paperback publishers produce covers which might just as well be blank.

Next, bookshops which want to sell as many books as possible always stock their books face on or face out so that the front cover of the book is fully visible. Look in any remainder shop or in a bookshop (such as at a railway station, supermarket or petrol station) which relies on a fast turnover of books and you will see that they stock a high proportion of their titles face on. As I explained earlier experienced authors know how important it is that their books are displayed face on and so in large bookshops (particularly in certain parts of London) you will see authors furtively moving their books from bookshelves (where they are displayed with only the spine visible) to a display table (where the whole of the front cover can be seen). Not surprisingly, bookshops will not be enthusiastic about displaying a book face on if the cover is not attractive.

You may, at some time, want to use a photograph of your book cover in a catalogue. Or, if you are lucky enough to persuade a newspaper or magazine to review your book, they may want to reproduce the cover. If the cover is attractive then this will help to sell your book. If the cover is dull, boring and unattractive then a photograph of the cover could well be more of a hindrance than a help.

While on the topic of newspaper and magazine reviews it is worth mentioning that editors who are reviewing half a dozen books will often select just one cover to illustrate their feature. Editors as a breed may not be among the brightest people in the world but most are equipped with enough native cunning to realise that their page will look bright and attractive if they choose the most attractive and exciting cover available to them. If your book cover looks like the front of an old-fashioned telephone directory your book will be unlikely to receive this extra boost.

Next, even if you sell your books by mail order if your book looks uninspiring, miserable and second rate the reader who takes your book out of the padded bag will be disappointed. And, being disappointed there is naturally a greater chance that he will not like your book. If he doesn't like your book he may send it back and ask for a

---

PRODUCTION TIP

SHOULD YOU PUT YOUR PRICE ON THE COVER?

Don't have your book price printed on your book unless you are feeling very confident. If you print a price on a book cover and you want to increase the price then you will have to have a lot of stickers printed. And then you will have to find someone to stick them all on. And then someone will complain that you have increased the price of your book and you will probably get into trouble. There is bound to be a quango somewhere which does not approve of raising prices. (Such bodies are not infrequently manned and womanned by people who never actually have to dirty their hands with anything so distasteful as having to earn a living.)

On the other hand, if you are feeling confident, putting a book price on a cover does have one big advantage: if you want to sell the book at a cheaper price your customers will be able to see exactly how much money they are saving.

refund. If this happens you will lose money because you will have paid to post the book to him and when the book comes back it will probably not be resaleable; he will obviously not recommend your book to anyone else (and since word of mouth recommendation is by far the best and most effective long term method of selling books you will therefore suffer commercially) and he is extremely unlikely to become a faithful customer.

Finally, authors always complain when publishers give their books rotten covers. So authors who publish their own books owe it to themselves (and to their books) to give them good covers. Besides, if you are proud of the way your book looks you will be much more enthusiastic about promoting it. If you feel rather ashamed of its seedy appearance you will not be able to do your book justice.

7. HOW MANY SHOULD YOU PRINT?

Once you start getting quotes from printers you will be astonished to see just how cheap books can be when you order large quantities. If you order 500 copies of a book then each copy may cost you, say, £6. If you order 1,000 copies then each copy may cost you £4. Were you to order 5,000 copies then it is a fair bet that the unit price would crash to £1.50 each. And if you were to rashly order 10,000 copies then it's likely that you would pay only around £1 each. A print order of 100,000 (if you ordered this many you would probably have to requisition every spare bedroom and garage in your neighbourhood for storage space) would bring your unit price down to a point where it could be measured in pence.

The reason for this is obvious. The biggest cost in printing a book is getting the

---

PRODUCTION TIP

'SHORT RUN' PUBLISHING

You may decide that a few hundred books is all you need. You might be publishing a high price book with a guaranteed, but small, customer base. Or you may simply want to keep a successful book in print as a backlist title (knowing that you can sell a small, but worthwhile, number of copies each year). A growing number of print companies are now able to produce short runs of books at a viable unit price. (It is probably fair to say that anything less than 1,000 copies of a book is a 'short run'.) Instead of tying up space and money in too much stock it might be worthwhile discussing this short run option with your printer.

book ready for the printing presses. Once the presses are rolling the cost of additional paper and the cost of allowing the presses to run for a short while longer is relatively small.

You should try hard to resist the temptation to attempt to bring down the unit cost of your book by printing more than you realistically think you will be able to sell.

Even if you are convinced that you have a sure-fire winner you should be cautious. Do not be embarrassed or ashamed to print just 1,000 copies of your first edition. Indeed, I would strongly suggest that your first print order should be no more than 1,000 copies of your book.

On two occasions I have allowed my enthusiasm to push me into printing more books than I should have. On both occasions the books were non fiction books published under the *European Medical Journal* imprint. On both occasions I was convinced that the books would be a huge success.

When I had finished writing *Power over Cancer* I was extremely excited. The book contained easily readable evidence showing readers exactly how they could avoid 80% of all cancers. It seemed to me that this was a book that everyone would want to read. And so I thought I was being pessimistic and cautious by limiting my initial print run to 3,000 books.

I then compounded that mistake by spending a relatively large amount of money promoting the book.

Today, when I begin an advertising campaign I start with just one advertisement. If the advertisement works then I will put the same advertisement into another newspaper or magazine. But if the advertisement doesn't work (by that I mean it doesn't at least cover its costs) then I will abandon it and try something different.

When *Power over Cancer* came from the printers I was desperate to get the book to as many people as possible. I believed that the book gave me a genuine chance to cut the incidence of cancer. I, and I think everyone else at Publishing House, felt excited by the book.

And so I arranged for advertisements to be put into several newspapers and magazines without any testing. To make things even worse I sent off 28,000 copies of a direct mail 'selling letter' promoting *Power over Cancer* to readers on our mailing list. I simply didn't want to waste any time getting the information in *Power over Cancer* to as many people as possible.

(As with advertising space bought in newspapers and magazines it is essential to test direct mail selling letters. We normally do test mailings of 4,000 names. Some, more cautious, mail order sales people prefer to test on 1,000 or even 600 names. Sending a leaflet to 28,531 people cost £9,985.85 so we clearly needed to sell around 1,000 books at £9.95 to cover the cost of the mailshot alone. Spending such a lot of money on an untested mailshot was poor judgement.)

The attempts to sell the book were a disaster. We lost money on every advertisement we bought and we lost money on the mailshot. As far as the mailshot is concerned we were saved only by the fact that we had routinely included a copy of our catalogue with the selling letter for *Power over Cancer*. We received a good response to the catalogue and this paid for the cost of the stamps and the mailing.

Nothing saved the press advertisements from failure. An advertisement in *The Daily Telegraph* which cost £1000 (plus the cost of preparing the advertisement) brought in a grand total of £318 worth of orders. Out of that £318 we had to pay for the books we sent out and the postage to send out the books. An advertisement in *The Guardian* cost £450 and brought in £109. An advertisement in *The Independent* cost £450 and brought in £189. And an advertisement in the magazine *Prima* cost £600 and brought in £199. Further advertisements proved to be just as disappointing.

And even when I tried to sell the book through my newspaper column the book was a failure. We sold 229 copies of *Power over Cancer* at £9.95 through my column. In comparison we sold over 700 copies of *Food for Thought* and over 750 copies of *Relief from Irritable Bowel Syndrome* at the same price.

If *Power over Cancer* had been my first venture into publishing and I had not had the income from other, more successful books to help pay for this disaster my recklessness in not testing the book properly could have put an end to my publishing career.

We have slowly (over more than two years) got rid of most of the 3,000 copies of *Power over Cancer* that were printed but the book has not been a commercial success and if I keep it in print I will have to subsidise it.

Our other notable failure has been *How To Stop Your Doctor Killing You*. This time I was convinced that the title would be a winner. Everyone who saw the book cover seemed to think it was bound to be a success. (Maybe that should have warned me that all would not be well.) And overseas publishers often jump at the book when they see the cover – choosing to buy it even when I tell them that other, less exciting sounding titles, sell much better.

I printed 3,000 copies of *How To Stop Your Doctor Killing You* but this time I was more cautious about buying advertisements.

CHECK YOUR BOOKS

Don't Forget

When you receive your finished books from the printers open half a dozen packs and make sure everything looks OK. Check the inside pages and the covers or jackets. It's likely that in every batch of books you will find one or two that are 'printer's rejects', but a random check when the books are delivered will usually highlight any major problem. If you do find problems, either on delivery or as you use the stock of books, then you can claim a portion of the retail value (usually 25%) from the printer.

My initial advertising spend was just £1,700. This was made up of £1,200 for an advertisement in *The Daily Telegraph* (which brought in a total of £1,094) and £500 for an advertisement in *The Guardian* (which brought in just £278).

When looking at these figures you must remember that an advertisement that costs £1,000 has to bring in about £1,500 worth of orders before it becomes profitable because to the cost of the advertisement itself you must always add the cost of the books you are sending out, the cost of the postage, the cost of the padded bag and the cost of paying someone to type the purchasers' details into the computer, the cost of buying labels, the cost of sticking labels onto padded bags, the cost of putting the books into the padded bags, the cost of putting the cheques into the bank and all the relevant overheads.

Why were these two books commercial failures?

I'm not sure, though I have some ideas.

I suspect that *Power over Cancer* did not sell well because most people don't want to know how to avoid cancer. They don't even want to think about cancer. They would rather wait until they get it and then rely on doctors to cure it for them with drugs, surgery and radiotherapy.

And I suspect that *How To Stop Your Doctor Killing You* flopped because most people don't like to think that their doctor is an incompetent buffoon who is likely to kill them (even though the facts show that this is the case). Most people may accept that other people's doctors are buffoons but they prefer to think of their doctor as a wise man whom they can trust and who will save their lives through his diagnostic and pre-scribing skills if they fall ill. As long as their doctor seems to know their name and smiles at them when they enter the consulting room they will trust him and do anything he tells them to do.

YOU NEED AN ISBN

DON'T FORGET

You will need an International Standard Book Numbering number (known as an ISBN) for your book so that the book can be identified by bookshops, librarians and so on. When you begin publishing write to The Standard Book Numbering Agency and they will send you a useful little booklet and a list of ISBN numbers for you to use. You may also decide that you need an ISBN bar code for the cover of your book. ISBN bar codes don't add a great deal to the design of a book cover but they are essential if you expect to sell a lot of copies through book shops. We used to put ISBN bar codes on all our books but have stopped doing this recently. We took this decision for two reasons: a) as we don't sell primarily through bookshops the cost of a bar code ISBN was an unnecessary cost and b) they make our covers and jackets look a mess.

I have published other books which have failed to make money. But I have usually known in advance that the books were unlikely to make money.

For example, when I published *Fighting for Animals*, which deals with animal rights, I was not surprised when I could not sell the books even when I discounted the price to £2.95 (at which point I was making a considerable loss).

Because I had published *Fighting for Animals* out of passion rather than out of any commercial logic I only printed 1,000 copies. Most of these have been given away rather than sold and as long as they are read that is fine by me.

My mistake with *Power over Cancer* and *How To Stop Your Doctor Killing You* was to print too many books. Over eagerness and over confidence increased the financial loss.

8. HOW MUCH SHOULD YOU CHARGE FOR YOUR BOOK?

The price of printing and binding your book is not, of course, the only factor you must take into consideration when deciding what to charge. You have to include costs for setting the text ready for printing (unless you have done this yourself on a computer), preparing and printing a cover or jacket, transporting and storing your books and, of course, marketing, promoting and selling your books.

It is this final item which most small, self publishers forget. The printer tells them that printing 1,000 copies of their book will cost £1,750 to print. They work out that this is £1.75 per book and assume that they can safely make a profit (or, at least, cover their costs) if they charge £2.95.

When they discover that their local bookshop wants a 40% discount and that the bill for printing a few leaflets and buying one relatively small advertisement in an appropriate publication will cost them £1,000 they begin to panic. The panic turns to terror when they realise that if they sell their book through the post they will have to give lots of money to the Post Office (which is always reluctant to give away stamps for free). And then there will also be the cost of buying padded bags in which the book can be posted. And there will also be the cost of paying someone to put the books into the padded

FINANCIAL TIP

MONEY TIP

If you have 1,000 books printed and your print bill is £2,500 then each book costs £2.50 to print. But the books will really have only cost £2.50 if you sell them all. If you only sell 500 books (and give away the rest or simply keep them in the garage) then each book will have cost you £5. Remember this when working out costs.

bags. And then there is the cost of hiring someone to stick the address labels and the stamps on the outside of the padded bags.

(I heard of one author who published 1,000 copies of his own book. The books cost £4 each to produce and he offered them for retail sale at £5.95. When a large book chain offered to buy 500 copies on sale or return but wanted a 50% discount he had to turn down the offer because he would have made a large loss on the deal. In my view either his print and production costs were too high or else his retail price was too low.)

The easiest way to save money is, of course, by not advertising and not sending out any leaflets or brochures promoting your book. This, more than any other reason, explains why so many self publishing authors end up with unsold stacks of books piled high in the spare bedroom and the garage.

***

Choosing a price may seem daunting but, as is the case with so many other areas of self publishing, other people have already done all the hard work for you.

The first thing you should know is that you should always end your price with the figures 95.

If you want to charge approximately £10 for a book then you should charge £9.95.

Don't make the error (made by so many big publishers) of charging £9.99. You may think that you will make another 4 pence a book and that if you sell 1,000 books you will add £40 to your bottom line profits.

This is a big mistake.

Book buyers will think of £9.95 as £9 (and therefore less than £10). But they will 'see' £9.99 as £10. And your sales will be reduced.

Take advantage of the years of research done by some of the world's biggest mail order publishers. Mail order publishers know what readers want because they get immediate feedback as a result of their advertisements and because it is possible to measure very precisely the success or failure of every book and every advert.

After experimenting with book prices mail order publishers have come to the conclusion that a book price should be one of the following:

• £9.95	• £12.95	• 14.95	• £19.95
• £24.95	• £29.95	• £34.95	• £39.95

(unless you are selling a highly technical book which is likely to appeal to a very small, wealthy audience the final three prices above are more suitable for a report or a set of tapes than a single book).

Don't ask me why these are the prices to choose. I don't know and I don't think anyone else does either. And it doesn't matter. I could give you all sorts of pseudo-logical arguments about why £12.95 seems close to £10 but £13.95 seems closer to £20 but life is too short to get stuck on trivia and commercial psychobabble. Just say a quiet "thank you" to the mail order publishers who have spent vast amounts of money experimenting in order to find the right prices.

You should not, in my opinion, consider a cover price of less than £9.95 for any book you publish. A rule of thumb that used to be popular among publishers many years ago was that you should charge five times the total production cost (including printing costs and overheads). Because of rises in other costs (in particular the percentage of the cover price that has to be given to the retailer and the wholesaler) this is now completely out of date and many publishers prefer to charge up to nine or ten times the basic printing cost. If this turns out to be too high you can always reduce it later. More importantly, you can reduce the price when you sell your book to special groups of customers. I suggest that if you want to reduce the price of your book when selling it on 'special offer' you take it down to either £7.95 or £5.95.

If you start out by pricing your book at £5.95 you will have no room to manoeuvre if you want to sell the book at a cheaper price.

DON'T FORGET

LEGAL DEPOSIT – WHAT YOU MUST DO

Publishers have a legal obligation to send one copy of each of their publications to the Legal Deposit Office of the British Library within one month of publication. Publishers of periodicals, journals and newspapers should deposit one copy of each issue.

Categories which are exempt from Legal Deposit regulations
Publishers are not required to deposit the following categories of material unless a written demand for them is made by the British Library:

♦ trade advertisements
♦ timetables of local passenger transport services
♦ calendars and blank page diaries
♦ blank forms
♦ posters produced for the purpose of elementary instruction

British Library Legal Deposit copies should be sent to: *Legal Deposit Office, The British Library, Boston Spa, Wetherby, West Yorkshire LS23 7BY*

You must also supply Legal Deposit copies to 5 other UK libraries and these should be sent to: *The Agent for the Copyright Libraries, 100 Euston Street, London NW1 2HQ*

9. REGISTER YOUR COPYRIGHT

In order to register your copyright you must ensure that you put the appropriate wording on the title page verso of your book (see page 63).

If you look among the prelims in other books you will see that publishers use a number of variations on this simple theme. The words have a vaguely impenetrable air about them which suggests that they may have some standing in law. If in doubt add a few hereuntos and wherefores to your clauses. These can, I believe, be purchased second hand at very reasonable prices from solicitors everywhere.

In addition, I have also taken the precaution of registering trademarks for my name and the name of my main publishing imprint.

Finally, as part of the copyright establishing process, every time you publish a new book you must send free copies (known as legal deposit copies) to various major libraries (see page 73).

PART FIVE
HOW TO SELL YOUR BOOK

"A living is made, Mr Kemper, by selling something that everybody needs at least once a year. And a million is made by producing something that everybody needs every day. You artists produce something that nobody needs at any time."

THORNTON WILDER (THE MATCHMAKER II)

Getting your book printed is the easy part. As the publisher you will be paying out money and so you won't have much trouble finding a printer to make you some books.

Selling and distribution are the difficult bits of the exercise. As anyone who has ever bought and sold a house will know buying is much easier than selling. When you are buying everyone wants to be nice to you and to help you. When you are selling life suddenly becomes a good deal more difficult.

Most small publishers and authors who publish their own books make one big mistake: they spend most of their money on printing their book and allocate very little towards selling it.

Authors tend to be rather shy creatures and it may be rather nice to imagine that you can write a book, have it printed, stack the published volumes neatly in your spare bedroom and in the garage and then sit back and wait for buyers to beat a path to your door. Sadly, it won't happen. If you want to sell your books you have to put time, effort and (I'm afraid) money into advertising and promoting your book.

If you want to be a professional author/publisher my advice is that you should never spend more than half your overall publishing budget on printing. In other words you should never publish a book without being prepared to spend the same amount of money on advertising and promotion as you spent on printing.

1. BOOKSHOPS

You will hit your first snag when you try and get your book stocked by the bookshops. There are around 3,000 privately owned bookshops in the UK (plus all the chain book-shops, plus all the corner shops that stock some books) but half of these have a minus-cule turnover. Reaching the managers and buying departments in all these bookshops (and then persuading them to order your book for their shelves) is one of the most difficult parts of traditional publishing.

Large publishers maintain teams of sales representatives who trail constantly around the country calling in at bookshops and trying to persuade them to take copies of the books on their latest list.

All small publishing enterprises have tremendous difficulty in trying to persuade small bookshops to take their books.

We offer a very good discount (up to 50% depending on the number ordered) and we pay to have the books posted to the bookshops. In addition we take back any book which a bookshop orders and then decides it doesn't want. This means they can order our books without any risk whatsoever.

We spend a fortune on advertising (in one recent year of publishing we bought over £500,000 worth of advertising space in newspapers and magazines and bought a considerable amount of space in trade journals advertising directly to bookshops) but despite this bookshops are extremely unwilling to take our books unless they have been ordered specifically by a customer.

One bookshop once telephoned on a Monday to order a copy of *Alice's Diary* for a customer. On the following day they rang again and ordered another copy of the same book. We accepted their order and posted a second book. On the Wednesday they rang again. This time they had two orders for *Alice's Diary*. We posted them two books. When they rang on the Thursday to order another copy we asked if they would like to take a few copies on sale or return. We said that this would enable them to have a better discount, it would mean that they would be able to supply their customers immediately and, if they put the books on their shelves, it might mean that they would sell a few additional copies. Despite the fact that this involved them in absolutely no risk whatsoever (we would have taken all the risk by sending the books to them on sale or return – if they didn't sell the books they wouldn't have to pay us for them but could simply return them) they did not think that this was a good idea.

It is the attitude of bookshops (and small bookshops in particular) which explains why we (in common with a growing number of small publishers) sell many of our books by mail order. Even more frustrating as far as we are concerned are those bookshops who insist that our books simply are not available. We regularly get telephone calls from would-be purchasers who tell us that they have visited every bookshop for miles around

GET LISTED

Send details of your book to *Whitaker's British Books In Print*. Whitaker will list your book on their database. This is done free of charge and enables bookshops to find the book (and you) if a customer asks for it. A list of newly published books appears in the back of *The Bookseller* every week.

DON'T FORGET

SALE OR RETURN

MARKETING IDEA

Bookshops usually buy books from a publisher on a 'sale or return' basis. What this means is that if the bookshop can't sell a book they will send it back to the publisher and demand a refund. They will either expect a refund in cash or in the form of other, different books which they can try to sell.

Naturally, most publishers prefer to sell a book on a 'firm' sale basis as often as possible since this means that the bookseller cannot return the book if he doesn't manage to sell it. It is often better to give a bookshop a larger discount for a firm 'no returns' payment than to insist on a smaller discount and allow the bookshop to return the book if they don't sell it. Books which are returned by bookshops are often unsaleable since they may be battered and have torn covers.

The saddest thing about the 'returns' policy as practised by many book-shops today is that books are given such a short time to succeed. Some bookshops now send books back after they have had them on display (un-sold) for a week. Three months is probably more usual but even three months isn't very long – it certainly doesn't give a book much of a chance to sell by 'word of mouth'.

---

and been told that *Alice's Diary* (or whatever other title they are asking for) does not exist. All our books are listed on computers, microfiche and in every reference book we can find; we sell thousands of books and advertise widely, regularly and expensively. And still there are bookshops who insist that our books don't exist!

***

Bookshop owners and managers (and bookshop assistants) often like to give the impression that they are providing society with a very special service. But the simple truth is that bookshops are no more than ordinary retail outlets, and the importance of bookshops in the selling of books is rapidly diminishing. Within a year or two it's possible that bookshops will be little more than historical anomalies, visited almost exclusively by the curious, by history students and by those with time to spare.

Bookshops will not be put out of business by the Internet (though some book-shop owners, mistakenly assuming that selling books this way is a major threat to their existence are already setting up their own subsidiaries on the Internet) because the Internet is at the moment an over-hyped piece of technological nonsense which is viewed only by a dramatically limited number of computer users, most of whom are nerds who wouldn't know how to open a book if you handed them one.

PAYMENT IN ADVANCE

FINANCIAL TIP

It's a good idea to ask for payment in advance if you haven't done business with a bookshop before. Small bookshops seem to go 'bust' with frightening frequency and bad debts can be a serious problem for the small publisher. Since many (or even most) of your sales will have resulted from customers walking into the bookshop and ordering your book it is perfectly reasonable to get the money from the bookshop before you send out the book. This process is often known as ordering on a 'pro forma' basis and written requests for payment with order are known as 'pro forma' invoices

I am not denying that the Internet may one day prove to be a commercial success, or that selling books on the Internet may one day turn out to be viable, but what I do believe is that hardly anyone (with the notable exception of computer companies) has yet found a way to make money out of this much vaunted and wildly over-promoted selling opportunity. For the time being the Internet can be ignored. (I've already had one attempt at selling through the Internet. I'll have another attempt when people with access to more money than I have show me how to make it work.)

Bookshops (and, indeed, many orthodox, well established publishing companies) are being put out of business by mail order and direct mail book selling. Most of them don't know it is happening. And some of those who know it is happening are doing nothing at all about it.

2. MAIL ORDER

The book trade regards mail order and direct mail bookselling as so distasteful that it has, for years, more or less tried to pretend that it doesn't happen and that if it does happen it certainly isn't anything that a 'proper' publisher would want to be associated with. "He sells his books by mail order" and "He is a mail order publisher" are always used in a derogatory way.

To some people in the world of publishing and literary criticism it seems as if mail order sales somehow don't really count. It is as though selling books by mail order is cheating – rather like digging out the seam of a cricket ball or giving your golf ball a helpful kick if it has found an unplayable lie.

The large, colourful advertisements for bookclubs are tolerated on the grounds that they move large quantities of books. It is widely believed that they help to accustom non book buyers to the idea of books and some of the most naive (or perhaps 'stupid' would be a more appropriate word) authors, publishers and bookshops believe that

GET INTO LIBRARIES

MARKETING IDEA

It pays to do everything you possibly can to make sure that your books are available in public libraries.

There are special wholesalers who buy specifically for the library service. You should send details of your book to as many of these companies as you can. Not only will you be able to sell your book to libraries (via the wholesaler) you will also receive a payment each time your book is borrowed from the library. This payment is administered via the Public Lending Right service so make sure you register details of your book/s with them immediately after publication. The Public Lending Right office can be contacted at: *Bayheath House, Prince Regent Street, Stockton on Tees TS18 1DF*

There are other benefits to having your books on library shelves. If your book is borrowed and read a great deal it will eventually fall apart and have to be replaced. And if librarians see that one of your books is popular they will be more likely to stock another of your books.

You will also benefit because when lots of people read your books some of them will talk about you, and spread the good word, among their friends. They may even like your book so much they want to buy a copy of their own! For this reason we always include a section at the back of every book we publish listing books readers can buy from us through the post.

readers are likely to be encouraged to pop into their local bookshop when they see a bookclub advertisement.

I know that readers of ordinary mail order book advertisements go into bookshops to order books. But I don't believe that many readers will go into a bookshop to order a book which they can obtain at a vastly reduced price from a bookclub simply by filling in a coupon or picking up the telephone.

Those who sell books by mail order can take advantage of the fact that many people undoubtedly find bookshops daunting. Only a relatively small proportion of the population ever visit bookshops at all, but those who do know that it is often difficult to find what you want even when you get there, that there may be long queues at the check out desk and that ordering books can be difficult if not impossible.

As if all these advantages were not enough, those selling books by mail order often go one considerable step further and offer their customers a money back guarantee.

THE HIDDEN COSTS OF MAILING LISTS

DON'T FORGET

You might think that buying 1000 names would be a relatively quick and simple task. But be warned: there are lots of extras which you will probably have to pay on top of the cost per thousand names (for example, postage and packing, printing the names on labels or putting them on computer disk). You may also have to place a minimum order – often 5,000 or more names.

Here is a example of a data sheet you might receive when purchasing names:

MAILING LIST DATA SHEET

List of mail order buyers of books on trainspotting containing over 250,000 recent purchasers. Continually updated and MPS cleaned with an average spend of £300 per transaction. Multi buyers incorporated in basic list.

Selections available:

Sex, Geographical area, Age, Multiple Buyers, Credit Card holders.

Basic list costs

Rental cost	£95 per 1000
Selections	£10 per 1000
Mailsort	£10 per 1000
Labels	£ 8 per 1000
On disk	£10
On CD	£25
Print listing	£ 5 per 1000
Delivery	£10*

*For courier delivery or other non Royal Mail services please enquire for costs.

Minimum order: 5000 names

Delivery within 5 working days from receipt of order and payment.

All orders supplied for single use only.

3. DIRECT MAIL

In October 1997 *The Bookseller* (a magazine which is usually known as 'the organ of the book trade') published an article entitled *The Direct Approach* in which a journalist reported that: "Direct selling has been something of a fringe activity in publishing for many years. The main practitioners are the small independents with high-value niche books, for example publishers of technical directories, specialist financial titles or those publishing for the top end of the hobbyists market." I confess that this was not a description of direct selling which I recognised.

The term mail order selling covers all the different ways of selling through the mail (though it is usually used to refer to selling 'off the page' through newspaper and magazine advertisements).

But direct mail selling is very specific: instead of putting an advertisement in a magazine or newspaper (or on television or the radio or whatever other medium you can think of) the publisher sends a selling letter, together with a brochure of some kind describing one or more books, direct to people whom he thinks (or hopes) might be interested in buying from him.

If you decide to try direct mail then your biggest problem will be, of course, finding the names and addresses. There are several ways in which you can do this.

The first and cheapest is to compile your own list. Every time you sell a book you should keep the name and address of the customer. You can either write the names and addresses down in a little notebook or you can store them on a computer. The former is pretty useless. The latter is very useful.

Once names and addresses are in a computer (assuming that they have been stored in a special program which allows you to sort and select them) you can print out labels whenever you want. If you have a purpose built program you can print out the names and addresses of all the men living in Wales who have bought your book entitled *Rock Climbing In The Welsh Valleys*. You can then send them details of your new book entitled *More Rock Climbing In The Welsh Valleys*. If your brochure makes your book sound attractive, and you are selling it at a good price, your mailshot should be successful.

At Publishing House we now have over 100,000 names and addresses in a special computer program which enables us to select different groups of people in different parts of the country for new mailshots. Most important of all the program we have bought enables us to ensure that we do not send details of a book to people who have already bought it.

If you don't have names and addresses of your own then you can either compile a list (by going through directories in your local public library) or you can buy a ready made list. Buying a list of names will cost you anything between £75 and £400 a thousand. You can buy lists of names through list owners, list managers or list brokers. Numerous companies produce directories of the lists they have available. You can probably buy a list of general practitioners over the age of 40 who enjoy holidays abroad. You can almost certainly buy a list of science teachers between the ages of 21 and 30. You can, in short, buy virtually any list you are ever likely to want or need. But you must always remember that the more you pay for your list the more books you will have to sell in order to make a profit. (See page 80 for The Hidden Costs of Mailing Lists.)

4. DIRECT SELLING FINANCES

If you venture into direct selling (as all author/publishers should eventually) by sending leaflets and catalogues out to potential book buyers you will soon realise that the price of your book has to be at least £9.95.

Buying a mailing list of names may cost you anything between £75 and £400 per thousand names. (The cost varies according to the list you are buying. By and large the more specific and exclusive the list the higher the price will be. If you are buying a list of names and addresses of people who have bought books on fishing within the last 6 months, who regularly visit Scotland and who have an annual income in excess of £100,000 then you must expect to pay a high rate. If, on the other hand you are simply buying a list of people who have bought something by mail order in the last three years you will pay far less.)

To this must be added the costs of writing, designing and printing a brochure, buying envelopes, having the brochures stuffed into the envelopes, having the labels stuck onto the envelopes and then having the stuffed, labelled and sealed envelopes posted to their destination.

All this will put the cost of your mailing up to an average of around 44 pence per letter. (It may be considerably higher if your brochure is large, colourful and expensive. It may be rather less if you cut your costs to the bone.)

A 3% response from a mailshot is considered quite good in the direct mail business. (For a cold mailshot – sent to people with whom you have never done business before and who have no record of having bought books by mail order – a 2% response would be considered fairly normal.)

So, let's look at some practical figures.

Assume that you send out 1,000 colour leaflets for your new book *How To Enjoy Skiing In East Anglia*:

Postage: (£200.00) + Envelopes: (£20.00) + Printing: (£220.00) = £440.00
Add cost of buying names at £200 = £640

If 3% of the people you have mailed buy your book and your book costs £9.95 your gross income will be 30 x £9.95 = £298.50. To this must be added the cost of printing the books and posting them out.

This is what is known technically as a "Whoops Oh Dear Response." You will have found a great way to lose money. And it doesn't even take into account the fact that some people will take advantage of your money back guarantee and demand a refund.

There is probably no way for you to cut your basic costs (you have to pay the Post Office, you have to have a leaflet printed) but there are three clear ways to turn this loss making situation into a profitable opportunity.

The first thing you can do is to try and reduce your controllable costs. Tell the people renting you the 1,000 names and addresses that you can't afford to pay £200 but that you will pay them £100 and, if your test works, you will come back to them to buy more names. There is a good chance that they will agree to this. And instead of having a colour leaflet get your printer to produce something printed in coloured ink on a good quality, tinted paper. This may help you cut 5 pence a leaflet off the cost of producing and sending out your leaflets. Your costs will now be cut to £390 (for printing and sending out the leaflets) plus £100 for renting the names and addresses of potential customers. Your total costs have been cut from £640 to £490. You have already saved £150 and things are looking much brighter.

The second thing you can do is to try to increase the number of people who respond positively to your leaflet and decide to buy your book. You can't do this by reducing your price because if you bring your price down you will have to sell even more books. And so the only way you can do this is to write a better leaflet.

The third way to try to make a profit out of direct selling is by increasing the price of your book. If you put the price of your book up to £19.95 and you still get a 3% response your gross earnings will be £598.50. The problem here, of course, is that in order to make your book look worth £19.95 you will probably have to increase your production costs fairly dramatically.

If you can do a little of both – get a higher response from the people you have mailed and put your price up a little – then your chances of success become higher.

So, for example, you might decide to increase the price of your book to £12.95 (at which level you can probably get away without any major change in your production costs) while at the same time improving your leaflet so that you get a 6% response from the people you have mailed.

Now look at the figures.

A 6% response will mean that 60 of your 1,000 potential customers each send you a cheque for £12.95. That will give you a total income of £777.

If you assume that each book has cost you £3 to print and that you have to pay another £1 postage and packing to send out each book then the cost of sending out 60 books will be £240.

Your total costs are, therefore, £490 (for the mailing) and £240 (for the books you sold). This adds up to £730. And since your gross income was £777 you have made a profit.

Congratulations. (But don't forget that if, say, two people don't like your book and ask for their money back your income will be reduced to around £750 – reducing your profit to £20.)

Now, a profit of £20 doesn't sound much for all that work.

But this was, after all, a test.

Your next move is to rent 4,000 names and do a slightly bigger mailing.

If that bigger mailing works you then continue to do more and more mailings.

If you can eventually mail 50,000 names with the same leaflet you could end up with a profit of 50 x £20 which is £600 and, I'm sure you will agree, a little more worthwhile.

But just imagine how difficult it would have been to make ends meet (let alone make money) if you had decided to sell your book for £3.95!

Writing A Direct Mail Letter

- ◆ Don't worry too much about grammar. Your direct mail should be easy to read. You're not trying to win prizes or impress the English teacher. You're trying to communicate with people.

- ◆ Make sure that your direct mail letter has a PS. An amazing four out of five readers will read the PS in your letter before they read anything else. So you must have a PS. The PS should summarise (very briefly) some key benefit or simply encourage the reader of your letter to respond. (As in: "Don't forget our solid gold guarantee means that you have absolutely nothing to lose and everything to gain by responding to this offer".) If you can think of an excuse to put in a PPS then do so.

- ◆ Tell a story in your letter. Write your selling letter as though you were writing to a friend to tell them about an exciting new discovery. Keep everything you write simple and easy to read. Avoid using big words which readers may not understand. Avoid too many adjectives and (especially) adverbs. Try to make sure that there is plenty of action in your copy. Some of the best and liveliest writing in Britain today appears in tabloid newspapers. Read the tabloids and absorb a little of the writing style the best writers use.

PRODUCTION TIP

CHECK YOUR TYPEFACE

Some typefaces work better than others for leaflets. Obviously whatever you use needs to be clear and so it's often best to avoid fancy lettering which can often be difficult to read.

And remember, too, that some typefaces print up better than others on the finished leaflet. Ask your printer for advice.

- Use testimonials and quotations.

- Use colour in your letter. Print some headlines in a colour, for example.

- You must sign every letter. But you don't have to sit there and sign thousands and thousands of letters. Give the printer a copy of your signature and ask him to add it to the end of every letter. And print your signature in a different colour to the copy of the text so that it stands out. Blue is a good colour for a signature.

- Make sure that you indent the first line of every paragraph. Some people think that justified text (a ragged edge down the right hand side) is easier to read and friendlier.

- Use capital letters only occasionally. If you want to draw attention to a piece of text use bold or underline the copy. Capital letters look as though you are SHOUTING and making too much of an effort. In headlines you should use upper case for the first letters of key words. Find the hottest benefit to the reader on each page in a leaflet and draw attention to that benefit in a headline. Put quotation marks around your headlines to make them more noticeable and memorable.

- Whenever appropriate and possible use lots of facts and figures to substantiate any claims you make. Draw attention to these with bullet points down the side of the text. (Bullet points have been used in this section of text and elsewhere in the book.)

- Use photographs and graphics wherever possible to liven up your pages. There should be a photograph of you (the author) and you should also reproduce your book cover. Remember that every photograph of an individual should be accompanied by a caption. So, if you have a photograph of yourself put your name under the photograph. You might like to add a quote if you can find one that seems suitable. (So, for example, if your name is Walter Wallkarpet and you have written a book on floor coverings and you were described by *Rug Weekly* as "Britain's best known and most knowledgeable carpet expert" you might like to put this quote (attributed) under your name.)

- Make sure that your leaflet is legible. Don't skimp on the ink. Your response will be around 10% higher if your printer uses lots of black ink (or, if necessary, prints the whole brochure in 'bold').

- Don't use full stops on headlines. You want your readers to keep reading. A full stop is likely to halt them in their tracks. And to keep people reading your leaflet make sure that you break the last sentence on every page of your sales letters. Just below the last sentence print: "Please turn to page 2" (etc).

- You must print a code on all your leaflets so that you know which mailshot produced which response. If you have a coupon on your direct mail leaflet then you can get the printer to print identification codes on different batches of the same leaflet. Before the leaflets are printed calculate how many you need with each particular code. Codes for monitoring responses are variously known as 'Key Codes', ' Source Codes' and 'Response Codes'.

PEOPLE BUY IDEAS AND DREAMS

MARKETING IDEA

The only two fundamental functions of any business (whether it be a professional offering knowledge or a skill, a service provider such as a hairdresser or an estate agent, a corner shop, a local business, a multinational business or an author selling his own books) are to create new products and to then sell those new products.

But people do not buy products or services: they buy ideas, hopes, solutions, time, concepts, entertainment and dreams. The woman who goes into a hairdressers salon isn't going there to get her hair cut. She is going there because she wants to look good. When people buy cars they are buying an 'image' as much as a means of transport. And the person who buys a book isn't buying a book but is buying information, education, entertainment or a gift. Remember this when you write your selling letters and design your advertisements.

5. YOU MUST HAVE CONFIDENCE IN WHAT YOU ARE SELLING

You yourself simply must know why whatever it is that you are selling is the best. And you must have confidence. Self belief plays a large role in success. This is true whether you are selling door knobs, motor cars, surgical skills, corsets, house building expertise or lawn mowing know how. You must not allow your potential customer even to think of finding an alternative. There must be no alternative. Your customers simply must have your product. Your service or product must be unique. (You can help yourself identify the sort of 'uniqueness' which produces success by looking around the world and identifying successful products and individuals. Once you have done this ask yourself what it is about those products and individuals which makes them so successful.)

What previously undervalued, unmentioned skills and advantages can you offer? Why should customers deal with you? What are you good at? What are the obvious – and not so obvious – benefits of their developing a relationship with you?

You must have confidence in what you are selling. If you do not admire the service or product you are selling – and genuinely believe that it is the best available – then your potential customers won't have faith either.

A Venetian nobleman once complained when a sculptor wanted to charge a hefty fee for a piece of work that was going to take ten days to create. "You forget," said the sculptor, "that I have been thirty years learning to make that bust in ten days."

Do not make the mistake of believing that you have to start with money in order to make money. You don't. You can make a fortune without having anything to start with. All you need are ideas and enthusiasm and ambition and self belief. Ideas are power. And poverty and riches are both the result of faith.

"He's lucky," people say. "Everything he touches turns to gold. I wish I had his luck."

They say this, often with rather more than a tinge of envy, about anyone who has been able to make more than one business venture succeed. Most people never even try – let alone make one venture succeed – and so they feel that anyone who is consistently or repeatedly successful must simply be lucky.

But luck has nothing (or, at least, very little) to do with business success.

Continued business success is a result of application, accuracy, attention to detail, planning, determination and reliability. Honesty, although not essential, is also pretty useful.

It was Burke who said, in the House of Commons in London, that he knew statesmen who behaved like peddlers and merchants who acted like statesmen. Whatever you do with your life you should always aim to act like a statesman. You may be able to make a lot of money in a short time by being dishonest. But you will not stay in business for long. If you want to keep on writing books – and keep on selling them – then you must be honest and honourable. There really is no other way. You must also be sincere, understanding and sympathetic to the needs of your readers.

And you should know that hard work alone is not necessarily the route to making money.

Never forget this simple, self obvious, truth: if hard work alone created wealth then on Friday evenings our factories and mines and office buildings would disgorge millionaires by the busload.

6. SELLING NON FICTION

The first and most important thing to remember is that you must try to forget that you are selling books.

Most people don't buy books.

Whether the book you have to sell is about trains, flower arranging, a cricket team on tour, mountain climbing, embroidery, murder on the Orient Express, irritable bowel syndrome or growing dahlias you are either selling information and advice or you are selling entertainment.

The remainder shops are stacked to the ceiling with beautifully illustrated, expensively produced books which were written and published by people who didn't understand that simple rule of publishing life.

If you try to persuade people to take out their cash, credit cards or cheque books simply to buy a book on flower arranging you will have a hard time.

So, if your name is Gertrude Bloom and you have just written a book on flower arranging how can you persuade a complete stranger (even someone who is enthusiastic about flower arranging) that they must buy a copy of Gertrude Bloom's *Complete Book of Flower Arranging*? How can you persuade them that their life will be incomplete without a copy of your valuable tome?

You have two primary choices (and the choice you make will, of course, depend upon the content of the book).

First, you can decide that you are basically going to sell advice and information.

You can tell potential purchasers that your book on flower arranging will tell them everything they are ever likely to want to know about the subject. You can explain that your book will tell them precisely what to do to produce a stunning arrangement. You can tell them that "the author has won prizes on three continents for her flower arranging skills". And all that will help to sell your book.

But if you are going to make your book about flower arranging a real bestseller you must understand what it is that your potential customers really want and need.

Now I know nothing whatsoever about flower arrangers or flower arranging but it is a pretty safe bet that most people who spend time, effort and money arranging flowers do so to please, impress and delight other people. If they arrange flowers professionally then they want their customers to be so thrilled that they rush and tell all their friends. If they arrange flowers for their own home then they will want to delight and impress their relatives and friends.

So, that is what you have to sell your potential customers: the prospect that they will, if they read your book, learn all the secrets about successful flower arranging and acquire astounding flower arranging skills. If they buy your book they will impress and delight everyone who sees their work.

If you want to sell your book through the mail by using newspaper advertisements, or through a leaflet which you deliver to potential customers, then you have to make sure that the advertisement or the leaflet define and draw attention to these advantages.

If you intend to sell your book through bookshops then you must make sure that the cover of your book tells potential customers exactly how they will benefit if they buy your book. It really isn't enough to draw attention to your skills and achievements. You must make it clear that the purchaser of the book will, by having access to your advice and information, become just as skilful and successful as she or he would like to become.

The bottom line is that if you are going to sell a non fiction book successfully on the basis of the advice or information it contains then you have to remember that you are primarily selling dreams.

Your purchaser has a dream (which you may have helped arouse through your advertising) and your book is designed to help them satisfy that dream.

Your second chance of selling your book on flower arranging is to sell it as entertainment.

The book may, for example, contain very few practical tips and hardly any useful secrets that will help the reader become a better flower arranger.

But it may be stuffed from cover to cover with your excruciatingly funny anecdotes about flower arranging. There may be page after page detailing your side-splitting experiences with fern, gladioli and chrysanthemums. You may spill the beans about your behind-the-scenes experiences among the world's top flower arrangers.

The book may, in short, be an exciting, enthralling and irresistible read for anyone interested in flower arranging.

Sadly, however, there is a snag here which may interfere with your sales. If you have printed a relatively small number of books your unit price may have to be higher than the average flower arranger will want to spend on entertaining him or herself.

For example, you may have decided to test the market by printing just 1,000 copies of the book. You cannot sell the book for less than £9.95.

And many of your potential customers will regard that as too high a price to pay for a few hours entertainment.

Your problem is that large, general publishers, bookshops and remainder shops – where books are routinely sold very cheaply – have devalued books and many consumers who would be happy to spend £9.95 (or more) on a CD or cassette tape, on a meal in a restaurant or on a theatre ticket, regard £9.95 as too much to spend on a book for themselves (despite the fact that they will obtain several hours of entertainment out of the book even if they only read it once).

So, do you give up?

Of course not.

Even though you know that many flower arrangers would love to read your delightful memoirs, you do not bother advertising the book to them directly.

Instead you advertise it to their friends and relatives. And you advertise the book as a gift.

Amazingly, there are thousands of people who have spent their lives in publishing and bookselling who still don't realise that most of the books which are sold are sold as gifts. Ask any bookshop manager when he sells most books and he will tell you that he moves most of his stock – and makes most of his profit – in October, November and December. He isn't selling books – he is selling Christmas presents.

It is, of course, far easier to sell a book for £9.95 if you sell it as a gift ('The Perfect Present For Any Flower Arranger') but if you decide to sell your book this way you may decide to print it not in a paperback edition but in a hardback version. The reason for this is simple. A hardback book makes a better and more 'special' present than a paperback book. It seems more valuable and makes a more impressive gift.

Naturally, since you are selling a hardback book you can increase the price to cover the increased costs. As a publisher concerned with making a profit you will, of course, increase the price by slightly more than the increased unit cost of printing a hardback book.

7. SELLING FICTION

It is widely believed that it is impossible to sell fiction by mail order or direct mail (unless you are selling through a book club and offering books at a heavily discounted price).

This is not true.

So far, I have printed over 76,000 hardback copies of my novels since I started publishing my own books. The usual price of our hardback novels is £12.95 (though *Alice's Diary* and *Alice's Adventures* are £9.95). We have so far sold around 65,000 of those books. (The other 11,000 are our stocks of several titles.)

How do you sell fiction as a self publishing author?

Here are some tips:

• When you've finished your novel ask yourself which group of people will be most interested in reading it. We have had success selling my book *The Village Cricket Tour* through advertisements placed in cricket magazines. And we've bought advertisements for *Alice's Diary* in magazines for cat lovers. The message here is simple: if you've written a novel about rambling then advertise your book in a magazine which is read by ramblers. If your novel is about a stamp collector try an advertisement in a stamp collecting magazine.

• If you write a series of novels then you only ever need to advertise the first novel in the series. There are now five books in my Bilbury series (*Bilbury Chronicles*, *Bilbury Grange*, *Bilbury Revels*, *Bilbury Country* and *Bilbury Pie*). The books sell very well. But we only ever advertise *Bilbury Chronicles*. We rely on the fact that people who have read the first Bilbury book will want to read the others. Similarly, we don't buy advertisements for *Alice's Adventures* but rely on the fact that people who have read *Alice's Diary* will want to read the sequel.

• Try to sell serial rights in your novel to a magazine. This will attract readers who will either want to buy your book or borrow it from the public library. When we sold serial rights in the Bilbury books to a women's magazine we arranged for them to offer the books to their readers at a discounted price. The magazine had a 'special offer' for its readers. The readers were offered a saving on the bookshop price. And we sold lots of books.

• Don't forget that most hardback novels are bought as presents. If you've written a novel about skiing try an advertisement in a magazine for skiers. But advertise the book as a present. (People who buy a skiing magazine will almost certainly know other people who ski.)

• When you have published more than one novel put advertisements for your books at the back of every book you sell. And don't forget to include your address, the price of the book and details of how to order. When people receive one of your books as a gift – and enjoy it – they will know how to buy others.

8. PROMOTING YOUR BOOK

Once you have written and published a book you have to promote it. I know that the idea of talking or writing about a book seems rather tacky and slightly distasteful to many authors but it is, nevertheless an inescapable part of the process.

It would, I know, be very nice if we could all write books and then sit back and wait for people to clamour for them. It would be wonderful if we could shyly push our books out into the world and then allow them to find their own readers.

Sadly, however, it doesn't happen like that.

Every year tens of thousands of brand new books are launched. Add those to the hundreds of thousands of back list books in existence and you will see that no book will stand a chance of finding any readers if it isn't promoted. Even eminent authors write their own puffs and blurbs and bombard their publishers with promotional ideas.

There are two basic ways of promoting a book.

The first is to rely on free advertising such as may be obtained through reviews, interviews, profiles, feature articles, book serialisations and so on.

The second is to rely on advertising which is paid for with hard cash.

There are advantages and disadvantages to both these types of advertising.

***

Twenty five years ago, when I first started writing books, publishers' publicity departments frequently sent authors out around the country on promotional tours. These tours usually involved 'media opportunities' of four main kinds: radio interviews, television interviews, interviews with journalists from local newspapers and magazines and giving speeches at literary luncheons and dinners. A tour would last two or three weeks

MARKETING IDEA

LOCAL PUBLICITY

Obtaining publicity in your local newspaper and on your local radio and television stations should not be too difficult. Simply send them an advance copy of your book together with a press release explaining that you live in their catchment area. You may have to follow up with a telephone call but the chances are good that they will chase after you.

Having your photograph and a small feature on page 35 of your local newspaper will at least be a start. And a two minute spot on the local TV news will make you something of a temporary celebrity in the shops you visit regularly.

But, sadly, I must warn you that local publicity is not likely to sell many books.

> ## BOOK SIGNINGS — WHY YOU SHOULD AVOID THEM
>
> WARNING
>
> Many authors dream of sitting themselves down in a book-shop with a full fountain pen, a large pile of their own book and an eager queue of customers.
>
> Keep it as a dream.
>
> Book signings only really work for major movie stars who can attract a crowd simply by being there. Occasionally, famous or notorious authors can attract a decent crowd if the right venue is selected. But the savage truth is, I fear, that there is not going to be a big crowd at Ye Olde Booke Shoppe in Bilbury when you turn up to sign copies of your new volume on the history of railway poster art in the Balkans.
>
> Let ego-laden big stars do the signings.
>
> You and I are authors. We just write (and publish) the books.

and consist of four or five interviews a day. At the end of one tour I had jumped onto so many moving trains that I was no longer sure that trains actually stopped in stations. Occasionally, a publicity department would send a 'minder' with an author. The 'minder', usually an attractive young lady, would introduce the author to the presenters and interviewers (as an experienced 'tourist' she would have met them on numerous previous occasions) and take the opportunity to 'sell' and book in next month's touring author.

After I had done a couple of dozen of these large tours (often for both hardback and paperback editions of the same book) I quickly became experienced enough to cram everything I wanted to take with me into a bag I could sling over my shoulder. I knew that I would be moving from hotel to railway station to taxi to radio station to taxi to railway station to taxi to television station to radio station to taxi to railway station to hotel and so on. Luggage simply made the whole procedure even more exhausting. The more successful a tour is the more one has to rush since the 20 minutes allocated to an interview spreads out to fifty minutes and eats into the time allotted for travelling to the next venue.

On one occasion the publicity department sent me with a young, beautiful 'minder' who was either unaware of the amount of jumping in and out of taxis that a promotional tour involved or else was too conscious of her appearance to let herself travel with just one bag. She brought two very large, very heavy suitcases and a collection of smaller shoulder bags and handbags. I have never in my life travelled with so much luggage. Even when going up to medical school for a term I took less. Inevitably, I ended up carrying most of her luggage while she trotted ahead with a shoulder bag and a smile, opening doors and waving at people. By the time I sat down to do my interviews I was sweating heavily and wheezing audibly.

These tours were, in those distant days, worthwhile because there were scores of local radio stations and television stations prepared to do interviews with touring authors. Radio stations in particular had to fill hour after hour with visitors prepared and able to talk about something of moderate interest to their listeners.

Touring authors were a welcome change from representatives from the Local Association of Insurance Salesmen, local politicians, the local doctor ("Today the doctor will be looking at piles.") and (usually in July) plumbers explaining how to avoid burst pipes during the winter months (plumbers were always far too busy earning big money to pop round to their local radio station during the freezing months).

A radio interview might be as short as two or three minutes or as long as two or three hours. Listeners would frequently be invited to phone in to talk to the author – not necessarily about his book.

All this publicity did help to sell books. One publisher of mine produced a report showing that the sales of my book rose in different towns and cities around the country as my tour progressed.

These days I doubt if such long tours can be justified. Most radio stations now play a great deal of music and very little speech. I could see the end coming in the early 1980s when I used to record health information spots for a large radio station in the midlands. The pre-recorded spots would be sent to other local radio stations around the country. I used to write and record ten or a dozen of these spots at a time and each one would be played several times during a day. In addition to receiving a very small fee my latest book was promoted at the end of each item. ("That was Dr Vernon Coleman, author of *How To Conquer Spots*, published by Verybigbooks at £1.95 and, in view of the amount of publicity it is receiving, available from a surprisingly small number of bookshops".)

When I started making these pre-recorded items each one would last three, four or even five minutes but slowly as the months went by the station asked me to make the spots shorter and shorter. Down they went. First to two minutes. Then to a minute. And finally to a maximum length of thirty seconds apiece, crammed in between the records and the hysterical disc jockey. This natural progression continued until the spots disappeared completely.

9. ADVERTISING YOU CAN GET FOR FREE

I am constantly amazed at the number of publishers who fail to take advantage of all the free advertising that there is around.

For example, a surprising number of publishers produce books which have absolutely nothing on the back cover. What an absurd waste of space this is. Watch people in a bookshop and you will notice that the back cover is one of the first places they look. You can use this prime site in a number of ways. You can use it to promote the author in some way (with quotes, reviews and a picture for example). You can use it to promote other books you have published. Or, you can simply use the back cover to promote the book itself. If you have reviews or quotes (even if they refer to another book) use them. If you don't have any reviews or quotes then don't for heaven's sake make any up (once you lose credibility no one will ever believe you again). Instead pick out sentences or paragraphs from the book which give potential readers a flavour of what to expect. Sometimes quotes from within the book are more powerful than reviews or reader testimonials.

When we first published *The Village Cricket Tour* we didn't have any reviews or reader quotes and so we used the following quotes from the text within the book:

Wodger won the toss for the first time since the introduction of the current lbw laws. He seemed more surprised than anyone and quite uncertain about what to do. "What would you like to do?" he asked the opposing captain.

"It's your choice!" Tony Parsons pointed out. "You won the toss!"

"What do you think?" Wodger asked the rest of us.

"Let's bat!" said Oily.

"Let's field!" said Jerry, simultaneously.

We voted on it.

It must have been the first time in history that such a simple decision was taken in such a complicated way. By six votes to five we voted to field first.

***

Jerry's third ball was slightly over pitched and well outside the line of the off stump. The batsman swung as though determined to send the ball into orbit. The ball hit his front pad square on.

For a moment I didn't think Jerry was even going to bother appealing. When he did it wasn't so much an appeal as an indication of desperation. It was the sort of appeal a bowler makes and regrets a split second later; the cricketing equivalent of a grown up putting a note up the chimney for Father Christmas.

The umpire didn't hesitate. His finger went up as though string operated.

***

The ball soared higher and higher until I could hardly see it. For a while I watched it dispassionately, an innocent spectator bemused by this apparent denial of gravity. And then I realised that from the position my neck was in the responsibility for taking the catch would be mine. I looked around and, to my delight, saw that Norman, who was fielding near me, was running across to where I was standing.

"Mine!" shouted Norman, with uncharacteristic certainty.

I stepped back and watched him run forwards, his eyes fixed on the ball as it hung, apparently suspended in space.

"Yours!" he said suddenly, with equal certainty.

I snapped my head back and looked up. This time there was no mistake about it. The ball had finished toying with Isaac Newton's laws and was definitely earthbound.

***

We now have a huge variety of excellent reviews and reader quotes but we still use those quotes on the back of the book because I think that they give readers an excellent taste of what to expect.

Next, you should, whenever it is possible and appropriate, put advertisements in the back of your book. Publishers always used to do this but these days they don't bother. They either bind in lots of blank pages (what a waste that is) or else they simply throw away the pages they don't need for the book text (another waste). We always use every available page (that would otherwise be blank) to promote books on our back list.

Look at the back of this book for sample advertisements showing how we advertise our own books. (You will see other advertisement samples in the backs of most of our books!)

***

There are lots of other ways to get free advertising.

If you write an article for a newspaper or a magazine make sure that you ask the editor to allow you to mention your book at the end of your article. The article you write

---

WARNING

A WARNING ABOUT TELEVISION

Many television presenters seem to think that there is something distinctly tacky and unprofessional about allowing an author to mention the title and/or publisher of his book. Prior to arriving at the TV studios you may get a 'phone call from an exceedingly unctuous but at the same time pretentious person who will give the impression of being in charge of the whole TV programme and, indeed, quite a number of other important programmes. This person, who will turn out to be an assistant temporary junior researcher-cum-meeter-and-greeter at the TV station, will tell you that you will not be allowed to mention your book on air because of the station's policy. Pointing out that the station constantly carries paid for advertisements or (if it is the BBC) promotions for its own products will get you nowhere. There are two ways around this problem. If the programme is live then you can mention the title (and any other details which seem appropriate) as many times as you like before you are thrown off the programme and ejected from the studio. If the programme is recorded then I suggest you wait until about three minutes before the recording is due to start and then ask the producer to confirm that your book will be given a plug, either by the presenter or by you. If there seems to be any reluctance to mention your book you should ask about a fee. The producer will probably mutter something about paying your expenses. You should talk about your qualifications and professional expertise and suggest that a fee of £750 would be appropriate. Ask where you should send the bill. You will probably find that the reluctance to mention your book will suddenly and mysteriously disappear.

doesn't necessarily have to have anything to do with the book you have written. You are the link. Most editors will be happy to mention that you are the author of a book because this gives their publication a little extra touch of class. It is only a short step from getting a 'plug' for your book to 'selling off the page' by including details of how your book can be obtained by post.

(If you do this don't forget to include the price of the book, details of how cheques and postal orders should be made out and the address to which orders should be sent.)

And if you write a column for a newspaper or a magazine put a clause into your contract allowing you to sell your book(s) to your readers.

When I started to write the 'agony' column for The People newspaper at the end of 1992 I made sure that my contract contained a clause allowing me to sell my books, by mail, every four weeks. During the subsequent years we sold tens of thousands of books to readers of my column. Since there was no advertising cost involved in making these sales the profit involved was quite high.

10. ADVERTISING YOU HAVE TO PAY FOR

Free advertising can help you move a few books but unless you're very lucky (and there is always a large element of luck involved when you're trying to get free advertising since so many other factors can interfere with the amount of space you get) you aren't going to get rid of your print run with free advertising.

You are, after all, going to have to fight the fact that the bookshops are unlikely to stock your new book in decent quantities. Many and possibly most of your books are going to have to be sold through the mail. You are, I am afraid, going to have to become

DON'T FORGET

THE MEDIA BUYER

You may find that you can buy advertising space at below rate card by approaching newspapers and magazines direct. But you will probably find it easier to buy space through a 'media buyer' who will act as an agent between you and the various publications. The media buyer will cost you nothing. He will receive a commission (usually 10-15% and known as 'agency commission') from the publications in which you buy space. It's probably best to establish that the media buyer is happy to buy at short term rates. Remember, the lower the price you pay, the lower his commission will be.

If you decide not to use a media buyer then ask the publication to give you the agency commission direct.

a mail order publisher.

The single most important thing you must remember when buying advertising space is that you should hardly ever pay 'rate card'. (Rate card is the rate that the publishers of magazines and newspapers say they want to be paid when they sell their advertising space and this price is usually reserved for the exclusive use of banks, insurance companies, car companies etc.) Not paying rate card when buying advertising is almost certainly the second most important factor which will decide whether your publishing venture is a success. (The first most important factor is, of course, the ability to write a good, readable book that people want to buy – and keep.)

When you buy your ads you want to mop up the space that no one else wants. You want the advertising space that is left over at the end of the day and likely to go to waste if you don't buy it.

If a daily newspaper hasn't sold a chunk of space by 6.00 pm in the evening then they get very worried. And so they will sell it to you for a fraction of the price that they would have sold it to you if you'd wanted to buy it a week ago. A monthly magazine which is about to close its ad sales for the month will almost certainly have a few unsold spaces available which they will be happy to let go at a lower price.

Buying cheap, left-over advertising space is known, in the trade, as buying 'short term' (or 'distress') space. And virtually every magazine and every newspaper in the entire universe will sell 'short term' (though many of them will deny it). Posh newspapers sell 'short term'. Posh magazines sell short term. No newspaper or magazine publisher likes having to put one of those public service ads onto money earning space. No newspaper or magazine publisher likes having to run an advertisement for another product in their own group. It is an insult to the advertising director and embarrassing to the publisher. They would much, much rather get a real advertisement from you and put some money in the bank

Short term advertising space is the saviour of the mail order publisher. It is common to buy space at between a quarter and a third of the rate card price. I have, on occasion, bought advertising space at less than 10% of the rate card price. This tip should enable you to recover the cost of this book many times over when you book your very first ad.

***

Of course, before you start buying advertising space you have to have an advertisement. You have to have something to put in the piece of space you've bought. Read the notes I've made on this subject before you try writing your first advertisement.

Mail order specialists writing advertisements always look at everyone else's advertisements. They look because they know that the best way to learn how to write an advert is to look at what other people are doing. They don't copy other peoples advertisements (that would be crude and it wouldn't work) but they do learn from them.

The big problem any mail order businessman (or businesswoman) faces when looking at advertisements is the fact that they don't know which advertisements make a profit and which ones make a loss. (Unless the advertisement has appeared before – which suggests that it does make money.)

So, to make life easy for you I've included in this book a selection of our advertisements. And I'll tell you a secret that is worth several thousand times the cost of this book: all of these advertisements have been profitable and successful.

Don't simply copy our advertisements.

For one thing our advertisements reflect our Publishing House style. You need your own style so that you stand out. (And our advertisements are, naturally, protected by copyright.)

Any decent writer can write good advertising copy. It simply requires different skills to writing a book or an article or a short story or a column.

You must first of all grab the reader's attention. You must then interest him in your book. Then you have to get him to want to buy your book. And finally you have to make sure that he acts – and that you turn his attention, interest and desire into action.

But if you can write then it is a skill that can be learned.

***

WRITING AN ADVERTISEMENT

WRITING TIP

1. When writing the body copy for your advertisement use the same sort of typeface that is normally used in editorial copy in that publication. You want readers to look at your headline and not be entirely sure whether they are looking at editorial or at an advertisement. Make a 'mock-up' of your ad and position it in the paper or magazine the ad will appear in. Does it look in keeping with the rest of the layout and typestyles? Can you easily read the headline?

2. Try using a 'dropped' capital letter at the start of your text. This will help draw the reader to your copy – and encourage him or her to start reading.

3. Don't put the price in big letters. There is plenty of time for readers to find out the price when they have read your advertising copy.

4. If you have a coupon in your advertisement (and most advertisers who sell by mail order believe that a coupon can be important) have a thin dotted line around it (with a small pair of scissors to show the reader what to do). Don't use a thick dotted line or else you will risk frightening off a potential customer.

5. Put a copyright notice at the bottom of your advertisement.

6. Don't be devastated if your advertisement doesn't work. As few as 20% of new mail order advertisements work. If your advertisement doesn't work try another headline or rewrite the body copy.

A SELECTION OF PRESS ADVERTISEMENTS

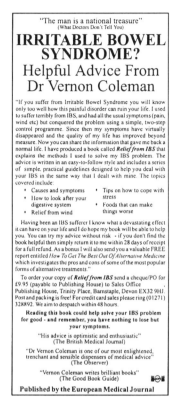

Note the use of the free gift in the IBS ad. Try testing your ads with, and without free gifts to see if this has an effect on response rate. If a free gift does pull in more orders, then try different free gifts until you find out what works best. Make sure your free gift is appropriate for the customer – and affordable for you.

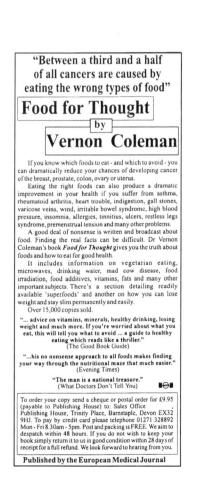

In the *Food for Thought* ad we have used a strong quote as the headline. Putting this inside quotation marks lends weight to the quote.

Note that both ads have been set in an editorial style which fits in well with the broadsheet press.

- Note the headline selling a gift – not a book.
- If you are using a coupon remember to find out where your ad will appear on. The ad above is designed for an outside edge position on a right hand page (so that the coupon can be cut out easily)

ONE OF OUR MOST SUCCESSFUL MAGAZINE ADS

Relief from IBS
£9.95 inc p&p

A sympathetic and practical book for those who suffer from irritable bowel syndrome. Full of advice and information you can use to help control and relieve the symptoms of this often distressing problem. The book examines the possible causes of IBS and offers an effective control programme which includes advice on: relief from wind - choosing the right foods - dealing with stress - building confidence and much more. Over 14,000 copies sold.

"I wish to thank you for your quite wonderful book which I fervently wish I had read years ago." (J.C., Port Erin)

"I've just finished your book on IBS and found it helpful and instructive. It's full of common sense material." (Mrs W., Devon)

High Blood Pressure
£9.95 inc p&p

It is estimated that upto 20% of the world's population have high blood pressure - of those only 50% know about it; and only 12% are being treated effectively. This comprehensive book covers the symptoms and causes of this extremely common problem. Dr Coleman also outlines his three-step control programme which can reduce blood pressure without drugs or doctors. Also covered is the role of doctors and how to get the best out of prescribed and alternative treatments.

How To Conquer Arthritis
£9.95 inc p&p

This book is quite simply a 'must' for anyone suffering from arthritis. It is clearly laid out, easy to follow and covers everything from osteo- and rheumatoid arthritis through to ankylosing spondylitis and gout. It is full of practical information which will help sufferers manage their condition and minimise troublesome symptoms. The list of topics covered includes: The facts about arthritis - what doctors can do - what you can do to help yourself - how to control pain without using drugs - when to exercise - alternative medicine - and much much more.

Food For Thought
£9.95 inc p&p

In this bestselling book Dr Coleman explains which foods are known to be associated with a wide range of diseases including: Asthma - Gall Bladder Disease - Headaches - Heart Trouble - High Blood Pressure - Cancer - Indigestion - and more. He gives simple guidelines for healthy eating and offers easy-to-follow slimming tips that can help you lose weight permanently. Over 20,000 copies already sold.

"I consider it to be one of the most brilliant books of its kind that I have ever read. Not only are the contents a mine of information and advice but the style is such that it makes the whole so thoroughly enjoyable to read; indeed it is a book difficult to put down."
(G.P., Streatham)

These are just a few of the books available by Dr Vernon Coleman. If you would like a full list of titles please write for our catalogue (a copy of which will be sent with every order).

✂ -
How to place an order - and claim your free gift!
Simply complete this form (block capitals please!) and send it with your cheque or postal order to: Sales Office _____ , Publishing House, Trinity Place, Barnstaple, Devon EX32 9HJ, UK. Please make cheques/POs payable to *Publishing House*. To pay by credit card please telephone 01271 328892 Monday - Friday 8.30am - 5pm. P&P is free. We aim to despatch books within 48 hours but please allow 28 days for delivery.

I would like to order the following books (insert number required in boxes)

Food for Thought £9.95 ☐   How To Conquer Arthritis £9.95 ☐
Relief from IBS £9.95 ☐   I enclose my cheque/PO for £ _____
High Blood Pressure £9.95 ☐   (payable to Publishing House)

Mr/Mrs/Miss/Ms _____

Address _____

_____

_____ Post Code _____

Treat Yourself!

Do you care about your health and the health of your family?

Would you like to feel:

Fitter • Happier • Healthier

Would you like to:

✓ Regain your zest for living
✓ Take control of your life
✓ Banish stress and anxiety

Then you need advice from "the patient's champion" Dr Vernon Coleman - the international, best-selling author, former GP and hospital doctor who you can trust.

Dr Vernon Coleman has been writing about medicine for over 25 years. He is well-known for his many campaigns in support of patients' rights and has received many awards in recognition of his work. Dr Vernon Coleman is someone you can rely on to give you the facts you need.

PEACE OF MIND GUARANTEE

All our books come with a rock-solid, money-back guarantee which means you can order today without risk. If you are unhappy with any book you order from us then simply return it to us in good condition within 28 days of receipt and your money will be refunded in full - no questions asked.

"Britain's leading healthcare campaigner"
(The Sun)

"His advice is optimistic and enthusiastic"
(British Medical Journal)

Free gift with every order
Free postage and packing

"Britain's leading medical author"
(The Star)

"The man is a national treasure"
(What Doctors Don't Tell You)

"Vernon Coleman writes brilliant books"
(The Good Book Guide)

TRADE ENQUIRIES WELCOME

© Publishing House, Trinity Place, Barnstaple, Devon EX32 9HJ
Tel (01271) 328892

- ◆ Note the prominent guarantee section
- ◆ This ad is designed for an outside edge position on a left hand page

102

A 'TRADE' AD WHICH APPEARED IN *THE BOOKSELLER*

You may want to advertise your book to the trade (bookshops, library suppliers etc). With such a large backlist of titles this ad was very worthwhile in terms of sales and raising the profile of the imprints.

Once you have created an advertisement and you are ready to start advertising you should always remember that by changing one small part of an advertisement you may be able to improve your response rate considerably. You might, for example, obtain a better response by moving or changing the headline, by altering the price or by offering a free gift. One of the reasons why it is vital to keep good records – showing the number of orders generated by every advertisement – is that it is only by keeping such records that it is possible to evaluate advertisements and compare each new advertisement with its predecessors.

It may take you a little while to find the right advertisement for your book – and the right place to advertise. (A good tip when deciding where to advertise is to look through a magazine or newspaper and see whether it carries any advertisements for books like yours – or for books at all. Then check to see if the advertisement appears again. If an advertisement appears more than twice then it is a fairly safe bet that the advertiser is making money.)

Don't expect to make a profit with your very first advertisement. But you will be extremely unlikely not to receive any money from an advertisement and since your overheads are likely to be low (and much lower than the overheads of a conventional publisher with smart offices in London, and the salaries of a regiment of marketing men to pay) you should be able to keep your losses to a minimum.

ADVERTISING TIP

DISPLAY OR CLASSIFIED?

When you start advertising in magazines and/or newspapers you will straight away have to choose between 'display advertising' and 'classified advertising'.

Classified advertising describes those pages of the periodical (usually at the back end) which include lots of small adverts (often for garden produce, rotary nasal hair clippers, loans and soft porn magazines or video tapes).

Display advertising refers to the bigger advertisements (usually at the beginning of the newspaper or magazine) placed by larger companies (such as life insurance companies, banks, motor car companies and so on). A display advertisement will be placed amongst editorial matter and can often be the only advertisement on a particular page (known as a 'solus' advertisement).

Classified advertising is usually cheaper than display advertising (even if you buy the same size space) but you pay for that usually modest saving: in our experience it doesn't seem to work as well.

My advice would be to steer clear of classified advertising if you can and buy the same sized space in display advertising.

You also have to advertise at the right time. Generally speaking most mail order specialists claim that the best months for advertising are January, February, March, September, October and November. The next best months are April, May and June. The worst months for mail order advertising are July, August and December. It is also widely believed that advertising on or around bank holidays is commercially dangerous. Our experience does not support these general rules.

If you can buy advertising space cheaply enough then July and August can be very profitable months for mail order sales. And though I would not try general direct mail marketing through the post during those months I might try direct mail to the over 50s in the summer on the grounds that it is people with children who are usually away from home then – and most likely to throw away 'junk' mail when they come back home and find the stuff littering their hallway.

Bank holidays aren't necessarily a dead loss, either. The success of an advertisement on a bank holiday seems to depend entirely on the weather. If you are a gambler or a weather forecaster with a good eye for accurately predicting the weather then you might like to buy a cheap advertisement on a bank holiday. If it rains then people will stay in and read the papers. And there is a chance that your advertisement could do very well.

(I should perhaps point out that there is always a danger that a big news story might destroy your hopes. If an eminent member of the royal family dies on the day when you have an advertisement running then you will, I fear, almost certainly lose most of your money. This risk is there whether you are buying short term or not.)

Of the first 16 advertisements which we bought for my book *Relief from Irritable Bowel Syndrome* just six made a profit. The profit we made on those advertisements just about balanced the losses we made on the other advertisements which hadn't worked. We were able to continue advertising the book because the profits were balancing the losses. But of the second 16 advertisements we placed 14 made a profit. We tinkered with the advertisements. We tried different magazines and newspapers. And we gradually bought advertising space at lower and lower prices.

We have since then noticed a similar pattern with other advertisement campaigns. Generally speaking our first advertisements begin by losing a little money or breaking even. But as we tinker with the advertisements and eliminate the magazines and newspapers which don't work we begin to make a profit.

Experienced mail order specialists claim that they aim to get a minimum of double their advertising money back in gross income. In other words if they pay £1,000 for an advertisement they want to sell at least £2,000 worth of books. That is a fine aim.

But authors who self publish and avoid the temptation to buy large office blocks in expensive parts of large cities can probably get by with a slightly lower return than this – though, naturally, it is always pleasant to do better than this. If you have a good product and you manage to buy a cheap advertisement you may be able to get a five fold gross return on your money – or even more.

ADVERTISING TIP

ADVERTISING TIP

VALUE FOR MONEY

Choose your position

If you can, choose advertising space in the first half of a newspaper or magazine (called, curiously, the 'book' in the business). Ask for an 'early' page (also known as 'front half' position). A right hand page will usually work better than a left hand page. And if you have a small advertisement try to be near the outside edge of the page rather than near the 'gutter' (where the fold, binding or staples are). If your advertisement has a coupon then the coupon needs to be on an outside edge so that buyers can reach it easily with their scissors. Remember this when you design your advertisement (it's no use designing an advertisement with the coupon on the outside left hand edge if you end up placing the advertisement on a right hand page).

Get Your Ad Ready In Advance

If you plan to buy at short term rates then your advertisements must be ready and waiting at the newspaper. If you are buying short term you don't have time to design an advertisement or get it set, printed and prepared. It has to be ready to be printed at a moment's notice. When you design your advertisement leave a space in the address line so that the newspaper can insert the response code for you. By doing this you can send the same advertisement to a number of newspapers and it can be re-coded each time it is used.

Getting A Re-run

If your advertisement isn't clearly printed or isn't in the position you agreed complain to the advertising department. If the error is a big one you can choose not to pay or to have the advertisement re-run. If the error is a small one you can ask for a reduction in the price.

Use Up the Leftovers

Companies will sometimes do amazingly stupid things when buying space. This is because they have far more money than sense. For example, a large company which is testing a new product may decide that it wants to advertise only in the South West of England. The newspaper then has to find an advertiser prepared to buy the same size space in all the other regional editions of the newspaper. Big, important companies may consider it beneath them to mop up this 'leftover' advertising. You will not. You will offer a ridiculously small amount of money for the space and get virtually national advertising extremely cheaply.

As a self publishing author you do, of course, have one enormous advantage over other publishers: you don't have to pay any royalties to authors. You're the author and the publisher and so you get to keep everything!

Tips For Writing Ads That Work

1. You must know who is going to buy your book.

You must know exactly who you are aiming at. When you first start selling your book you will have to rely more on instinct than anything else. Who do you think is most likely to buy your book? If the book is about trains then it is a fair bet that people who like trains will want to buy your book. If you've written a science fiction novel then you are probably safe in assuming that people who read science fiction will be your best customers. If you've written a romantic novel then you will probably do better advertising your book to women than to men. As you begin to sell books so you will learn more and more about your readers/customers. As the months go by try to build up a profile of your average customer. Male or female? Young or old? The information you collect will enable you to target your advertisements more accurately – both in terms of the form they take and the words you use and in choosing the right places to put your advertisements.

2. Decide why people should buy from you.

Tens of thousands of books are published every year. What makes your book special? Why should someone buy your book in preference to any other book? If you don't know exactly what it is you have to offer that makes you and your book unique then potential readers won't know either. A money back guarantee doesn't make you special. Nor does 'free postage and packing'. You have to be able to offer readers something that no one else can offer them. And you must remember that although you may be able to sell a few books to friends and relatives, simply because they know you and want to help you, people out there in the real world won't buy your book because they feel sorry for you or because they want you to succeed as a self publisher. Remember that would be customers want to know what is in it for them if they buy your book. When writing an advertisement you must put yourself in the shoes of your potential customers. Your customers aren't interested in the fact that you have published your

THE TWO MOST POWERFUL WORDS

The two most powerful words in advertising are:

FREE   and   **YOU**

ADVERTISING TIP

book instead of buying a new car. They don't care about the fact that you stayed up nights to complete the book. They will not be encouraged to buy your book by the fact that it is beautifully bound, or stored in a centrally heated bedroom or even by the knowledge that if you don't sell lots of books you are going to have to stick with the job at the bank until you retire. Many advertisers make the mistake of trying to sell themselves or their company when writing their adverts. They show a picture of their smart new factory or their fleet of vans because they are proud of what they have achieved. But none of this is of any interest or benefit to the customer. People don't buy a video recorder because it is made in brand new factory which looks smart in the brochure photographs. They buy a video recorder so that they can record television programmes as simply and easily as possible. People don't buy a novel because it took you three years to research. They buy a novel because they want to be entertained and because you have convinced them that your novel will entertain them. (Or they might buy it because they are looking for a suitable present for Uncle George and your advertisement has convinced them that your book is something he will love.) Arthritis sufferers won't buy a book on arthritis because it is printed on acid free paper and contains 267 pages. But they will buy a book on arthritis which they believe will tell them how to deal with the pain and stiffness of their arthritis. Before you write your advertisement ask yourself what it is that your potential buyers really want – what will make them want to buy your book. How will people benefit by responding to your advertisement? In what way will their lives be better as a result of sending you their money? You must offer the reader a solution to a problem he might not even know he has. After you have written your advertisement read it again and see whether or not you think it will excite a potential customer enough to encourage him to give you his money for your book.

ESTABLISH YOUR CREDIBILITY

If you are an expert and your book is about the subject of your expertise then you must establish your credibility in your advertisement. Give details of your qualifications, achievements and honours.

Don't Forget

---

3. Don't try to be too clever.
Advertisers and advertising agencies who want to win prizes often produce wonderful looking adverts. But big advertisers who rely on retail sales don't have a quick way of testing whether or not their ads have worked. And so they are likely to waste a great deal of money on ineffective advertising. Mail order advertisers, on the other hand, will know within a day or two of an ad appearing whether or not it is going to make money. So when you are planning your first ads take a look at the mail order ads rather than the fancy, clever ads. Mail order ads look the way they do because they work.

4. Your ad must be eye-catching.

We are all constantly exposed to advertisements. We ignore most of them and train our eyes to slide past anything that doesn't truly grab us. If you are advertising in a newspaper or magazine you have just over a second to catch the reader's eye and so if your advertisement is going to work it must contain something (possibly a photograph but

---

HEADLINES THAT SELL!

ADVERTISING TIP

The aim of the headline on your advertisement is to get the reader to read the rest of the advertisement. That's all. You can sell your book in the 'body copy' of the advertisement but the job of the headline is to draw in the reader from all the other distractions on the same page. If your advertisement is not read then you definitely won't sell your book and your money will have been wasted. Here are some tips to help you write a good, effective headline:

1 Try to reach out to readers – make your headline personal..

2 Don't be afraid to write a long headline. (But don't use more than 17 words in a headline.)

3 Put the headline within quotation marks. An advertisement headline seems to draw more attention if it is within quotation marks.

Headlines on advertisements and direct mail leaflets are as important as titles on books. Here are some advertisements which have worked:

- The Secret Of Making People Like You
- Five Familiar Skin Troubles – Which Do You Want To Overcome?
- You Can Laugh At Money Worries If You Follow This Simple Plan
- How To Talk To Your Cat
- When Doctors Feel Rotten This Is What They Do
- Read And Make Money
- Do You Make These Mistakes In English?
- Whoever Heard Of A Woman Losing Weight And Enjoying Three Delicious Meals At The Same Time?
- Discover The Fortune That Lies Hidden In Your Salary
- How I Improved My Memory In One Evening
- Do You Do Any Of These 10 Embarrassing Things?
- Imagine Me...Holding An Audience Spellbound For 30 Minutes

MAGIC WORDS

Some words have a magical effect when included in advertisements. Here is a list of some of the words and phrases which can turn an advertisement into a success:

ADVERTISING TIP

free	now	send for	the best	special offer	protect
how	win	find out	success	claim your	life
new	buy	secrets	power	announcing	sale
easy	today	how to	hurry	amazing	how would
complete	yes	make money	easy	facts	love
exclusive	save	learn	amazing	breakthrough	bargain
original	guarantee	discount	quick	at last	do you
you	learn	you too	bargain	advice	discover.

---

more commonly a headline) that is irresistible. A good, catchy headline should contain no more than 15 to 17 words and should make the reader want to know more. Your headline should make the reader curious and, ideally, at the same time promise the reader something he can't resist. An effective headline does not necessarily have to refer to the book you are selling but it should engage the reader's emotions and make him or her want to read more. For example, if you are selling a book aimed at back sufferers you might grab your reader with the simple two word headline 'Back Sufferers'. This would attract the reader's attention. And then, underneath this, you could add the three words 'Relief at last!'. This would, hopefully, ensure that the reader became interested and wanted to read on. Your task in the rest of your advertisement would be to turn his interest into a sale. If you are selling a book which you know will be bought as a Christmas present you could use the headline 'Your Christmas Present Problems Solved!' to attract would-be buyers to your advertisement. Remember, headlines seem to work better when they are put within quotation marks.

5. Your advertisement must be well written.

Writing advertisements that sell books requires just as much skill as writing books that sell. If an advertisement is to work it must be well written, convincing and easy to read. The text of the advertisement must maintain the interest triggered by the headline. You have to be careful with humour when writing an advertisement. Not every potential buyer has a good (or even any) sense of humour. And don't try to be too clever with sophisticated layouts or fancy typefaces.

6. Use testimonials.

If all goes well you will, within a fairly short period of time, begin to receive lovely letters from some of the people who have bought your book. You can use extracts from these

ADVERTISING TIP

MORE ABOUT RESPONSE CODES

As with direct mail leaflets you must make sure that each advertisement you insert contains a code – preferably in the address to which readers reply. So, for example, you might invite readers who want to buy your book from your first advertisement in the Daily Telegraph to write to Dept DT1 whereas you might invite readers responding to an advertisement in The Guardian to write to Dept G1. Putting codes on your advertisements is vital. Without codes you won't be able to identify the sources of your orders – and you won't know which advertisements have worked and which have not.

letters to help give your advertisements credibility. (Before you use names you must, of course, write and ask the letter writer for permission. If you simply use initials – and disguise them – then it probably isn't necessary to obtain permission.)

7. Don't go over the top.

Potential buyers simply won't believe you if you promise too much. If you announce that your novel is 'the greatest story ever written' you will lose credibility – and sales. Boast that your book will help people live to 150 years of age and readers will turn over the page and ignore the rest of your advertisement.

8. Make it easy for customers to buy your book.

You would be surprised how often mail order advertisements appear without the name and address of the seller. Your advertisement must include your name and address, the price of your book, whether there is any extra charge for postage, what guarantee you are offering, who to make the cheque payable to and, if there isn't a coupon to fill in, a reminder to them to include their name and address when they write to you. If you take orders by telephone then you should obviously include your telephone number. If you take orders by fax then include the fax number. If telephone calls are answered by a real, live person during normal office hours then say so – and spell out your version of 'normal office hours'. You need your customers to give you their name and address and, if they are paying by credit card, their credit card details. You must tell them how long they are likely to have to wait for their book ('We aim to send out all books within 48 hours but please allow 28 days for delivery) or else customers will be ringing up after three days to accuse you of stealing their money and to complain that they haven't yet received their book. If you are a member of the Mail Order Protection Scheme (MOPS), and your advertisement falls within the scope of the Scheme, then you must include the MOPS logo. You should not use the logo unless you have paid to join the Scheme. Remember that some ads are exempt from MOPS. (See page 117.)

ADVERTISING TIP

ONCE ISN'T ENOUGH

Remember to include the title of your book (and the price) together with your address and telephone number on every piece of mailing literature you send out. And if you publish an advertisement which contains a coupon repeat the details of where and how you can be reached outside the coupon. Just think how terrible it would be if you lost a customer who wanted to buy your book but couldn't because the coupon had already been clipped or the part of the leaflet containing your address had disappeared.

9. Words to eliminate.
When you have written your advertisement (or your selling leaflet) go through it and try to eliminate the two words 'that' and 'then' from your copy. These two words are grossly overused. They weaken strong copy and waste space.

10. Read your ad out loud.
Read your advertisement out loud once you've written it. This will give you a chance to spot any ambiguities, errors or confusing statements. If you can find someone else to listen while you read out the ad that is even better! And remember that the ultimate sin is to write boring copy.

11. LOOSE INSERTS

When you buy a magazine do you routinely lift it up by the spine, shake out all the loose bits of paper and throw them away without even looking at them?

Each one of those oh-so-easily abandoned inserts represents an expectation of success, a wild hope, or even a desperate dream for the mail order businessman who had the inserts printed and paid for them to be stuffed into the magazine.

There are three basic costs in buying inserts.

The first cost is in designing and having the insert printed. Since you will normally need to print at least 10,000 leaflets the cost of inserts is clearly quite high. You can cut the cost of printing leaflets by printing in huge quantities (for example, 100,000) which can then be coded in batches of 10,000. This means that you have ten batches of insert leaflets ready and waiting on the shelf. This is a good idea if you think you might want to put inserts into a magazine right at the last minute (when you will be more likely to be able to get a good price). If you need more than 10,000 you can use two or more coded batches.

The second cost is the amount of money you have to pay to the owners of the magazine to persuade them to put your insert into their periodical. This fee will be quoted as a cost per 1,000 and you should be able to get the price down quite a way from the original, quoted price. Only large companies with more money than sense (and advertising agencies keen to maximise their own income by paying rate card prices) pay the asking price. Don't pay much more than £20 a thousand to put loose inserts into a magazine. If you do then the chances are that you will lose money. As with display and classified advertising the cost of buying the right to put your inserts into a magazine will be lower if you buy the right at the very last minute. But to do this you will have to have your inserts ready and waiting to be sent to the magazine's printers.

The third cost is the cost of shipping the leaflets from your printer to the magazine's printers. Don't ignore or underestimate this cost. You will be moving leaflets in fairly large quantities. That costs money.

When negotiating the insert deal ask how many loose inserts the magazine allows. Three is fine, four or five is OK but if the magazine allows more than five inserts per issue then I suggest you look somewhere else. I fear that when a magazine greedily stuffs itself full of inserts there is a danger that the reader may not look at any of them.

If you are thinking of selling your book through inserts then your first task is to start collecting, reading and studying the loose inserts you might normally throw away when buying a magazine. The best way to learn how to write and prepare an insert is to look at as many examples as you can. (But you can make inserts work without spending a fortune on glossy, colour leaflets. We have always used black ink on tinted paper.)

12. RECORD THE RESPONSES TO YOUR ADVERTISEMENTS

It is vitally important that you keep a sales record for each advertisement – so that you can tell whether or not it was profitable. If you don't do this there is a real risk that you will continue to buy advertising that is losing you money.

We use a special mail order computer programme at Publishing House so that we can see at a glance whether or not an advertisement is working. And I transfer the basic figures into my hand held computer so that I always have a full sales record with me, wherever I am.

The two basic costs are, of course, the cost of buying the space for the ad (you can, if you like, add on the cost of having the advertisement made – we don't bother to do this because we produce the ads 'in house') and the cost of fulfilling the orders (this includes the cost of the book you sent out, the cost of the padded bag, the label and the postage, the cost of putting the cheque into the bank, the cost of paying someone to open the orders, sort the cheques, and put books into padded bags and the cost of fulfilling the guarantee by sending back some money to unhappy or dissatisfied customers later on).

One spreadsheet entry for a *Looking for a Present* advertisement looks like this:

Date	Autumn 1997
Publication	This England (magazine)
Ad size	Quarter page
Income	£1,979
Cost of advert	£1,200
Cost of bks/postage etc	£494.75
Profit/loss	£284.25 (profit)

And here is a spreadsheet entry for an advertisement which appeared in *The Guardian* for my book *Relief from Irritable Bowel Syndrome*.

Date	9.1.97
Publication	The Guardian
Ad size	20 cm x 2 column
Income	£845
Cost of advert	£300
Cost of bks/postage	£253.50
Profit/loss	£291.50 (profit)

Not all advertisements make a profit, of course! Here are the spreadsheet details for an advertisement for *Food for Thought* which appeared in the classified section of *The Times*.

Date	15.2.97
Publication	The Times
Ad size	20 cm x 2 column
Income	£368
Cost of advert	£523.60
Cost of books/postage	£92
Profit/loss	£247.60 (loss)

This system enables you to work out how many books you would have to sell to make a profit. And it also enables you to work how you much you could pay for another advertisement – and still hope to make a profit on that advertisement too.

If you keep a daily record of sales you will, after a few advertisements have appeared, be able to work out whether or not an advertisement is going to work after it has been running for no more than a day or two.

So, for example, we have discovered that if we have an advertisement in a newspaper on a Sunday then our total income from that advert is likely to be between 5 and 6 times the amount of money we take on the Tuesday after the advertisement appeared.

13. LAWS, REGULATIONS AND REGULATORS

We live in a heavily regulated world. If you want to park your motor car you have to find a regulated parking place and pay the appropriate fee. If you want to travel you have to stuff your pockets with paperwork and documents proving that you are who you say you are and showing that you have paid for the right to travel.

It is, therefore, hardly surprising that if you want to publish and sell your own book you will have to deal with a variety of regulators.

You may feel that it is only fair that there should be some rules. After all, if there weren't any controls on publishing anyone would be free to write anything they liked about anyone else.

However, in our society the risk of an author saying unfair or unjustifiable things about someone (or some organisation or limited company) is restrained by the existence of our draconian libel laws.

I do not intend to attempt to deal with the risk of libel in detail here. Men and women who spend their entire lives working with the libel laws often admit that this is an area of the law where good sense does not play a prominent role. "In most areas of the law it is safe to say that in nine out of ten cases the outcome will satisfy the rules of common sense," said one lawyer. "But in the area of libel law these proportions are reversed."

Anyone who writes a book takes a risk that he or she will be sued for libel. If the book is non fiction then the risk is that real people who are mentioned in the book (or who think that they are mentioned in the book) may jump up and down and claim that they have been libelled. If the book is a work of fiction then there is a risk that real people who have names similar or identical to characters in your book may suddenly appear and claim that you have deliberately libelled them and made an attempt to wreck their lives.

Naturally, in these circumstances, the plaintiff (or, if you are really unlucky, plaintiffs) will claim that the book has ruined his/her spotless reputation, damaged his/her ability to earn a living and ruined his/her social life. Such absurd exaggerations are necessary in order to win a damages jackpot.

You may think that if your book is published by a conventional publisher you will be protected by the publisher. But you should not put too much faith in this quaintly old-fashioned and comforting thought. These days many publishing contracts seem to contain a clause which puts all the responsibility into the pocket of the author.

Under some circumstances an author can be worse off if his book is published by a conventional publisher. These days there is a real risk that the publisher will settle with the plaintiff, paying his or her costs, handing over a small sum in damages and dumping all the responsibility on the author's doorstep. This may then leave the author alone, friendless and out in the open. Worse still it is not unheard of for a publisher to then demand that the author pay his costs, the costs that have been paid to the plaintiff and the damages that have been paid to the plaintiff. The beleaguered author can then find himself being attacked by lawyers acting for everyone.

There is not, in my view, much to be gained by forming a limited company to publish your book. If the limited company doesn't have any money the chances are that the plaintiff's lawyers will come after you as the author.

Whether your book is published by a conventional publisher or you are publishing it yourself you can sometimes buy libel insurance. But my experience is that this is not usually a practicable option. I took out libel insurance for one of my early books and the premium was, I seem to remember, roughly the same as the advance I had received for writing the book. And even if you take out libel insurance there may still be risks. The insurer may refuse to provide cover for some parts of a book, or for some aspects of the contents. The insurer may insist that changes are made before your book is printed and published. If the insurer can prove that you knew that the book contained libellous material then the insurance may well turn out to be invalid. And the insurance contract will probably include a contract giving the insurer the right to settle with any plaintiff, paying costs and offering damages and an apology.

The best solution is, I fear, to go through your book looking for potential litigation (and remembering that it is the words and phrases which seem most innocent and innocuous which, in the end, always seem to cause the greatest trouble). Read what you have written and ask yourself who might be offended by it.

If you are writing fiction then you should take all the precautions you can to ensure that you do not inadvertently libel someone you have never even heard of. For example, if you are writing a novel about a specific place and the book contains a character who is a crooked policeman it would be sensible to check with the local constabulary that there is no one of that name in the area. If you write a book which contains an evil doctor you should obviously take the elementary precaution of checking with the General Medical Council to make sure that they do not have someone of that name (or a similar name) on their lists of people licensed to practise medicine. You can also check with local telephone directories to reduce the risk of litigation. Keep a list of everything you have done to make sure that you do not libel someone accidentally. Your precautions may not prevent a lawsuit but they may help reduce the size of the damages a plaintiff is awarded.

The number of ways in which an author can get into trouble simply by writing a book seems to grow every year. As with libel all you can do is to use your common sense, do everything you can to ensure that your book is accurate and include the usual warning at the front of the book.

In a work of fiction it is customary to include at the front of the book a paragraph in which the author points out that the characters in his book are not based on nor intended to bear any resemblance to any living person. In a work of non fiction it is more appropriate to include a paragraph in which the author warns readers not to take any notice of any of the advice in his book.

But although the law may offer many hazards there are numerous other possible ways to get into trouble by writing a book.

For some book publishers the two organisations which arouse most contempt are the Advertising Standards Authority (the ASA) and the Mail Order Protection Scheme (MOPS).

***

If you seriously plan to advertise and promote your own books it will not be long before you receive a letter from an organisation known as the Advertising Standards Authority (ASA).

In theory the ASA sounds like a good idea.

The public is exposed to a seemingly endless variety of commercial propaganda and if the susceptible and the naive are to be protected from exploitation the country needs a strong, independent watchdog capable of providing protection for innocent consumers from the most misleading and manipulative advertisers.

But is the ASA the watchdog the country wants and needs?

In June 1995 the small publishing house I run received a letter telling us that someone had complained about an advertisement for my book *Food for Thought*.

The unnamed complainant disputed the claim: "Between a third and a half of all cancers may be caused by eating the wrong foods. In his bestselling book *Food for Thought* Dr Vernon explains which foods to avoid – and which to eat to reduce your risk of developing cancer."

The complaint seemed easy to deal with.

After all many books, official reports and scientific papers have linked food and cancer. The United States Surgeon General has published a report suggesting that diet could be responsible for up to 70% of all cancers.

The National Research Council in the United States of America published a technical report entitled *Diet, Nutrition and Cancer* which showed that diet was probably the single most important factor in the development of cancer, and that there was evidence linking cancers of the breast, colon and prostate to particular foods or types of food. This publication reported that there were at least six international studies which showed a direct association between the amount of fat eaten and breast cancer incidence or mortality.

In order to support our claim that it is possible to reduce the risk of developing cancer by avoiding some foods and eating others we submitted a short but impressive list of basic references – referring to both books and scientific papers – and offered to provide a longer list if this was considered necessary.

But this time we hit another snag.

The ASA would not accept references.

They had, they said, read the list of references. "But", they added, "this list in itself does not constitute evidence."

We could not send original documents because much of the material had been obtained on loan from libraries and a telephone call to the Department of Trade and Industry confirmed our suspicion that it would be illegal (a breach of The Copyright, Designs and Patent Act of 1988) for us to provide the ASA with photocopies of all the books and scientific papers involved.

The ASA remained unmoved, simply insisting that: "it is an advertiser's responsibility to submit all such evidence as is necessary to support their claims".

As a health writer who has spent 25 years fighting to reveal the truth about medicine and health matters I believe that it is vitally important to teach the public about the links between food and cancer.

But in February 1996 the ASA confirmed that they had recommended to their Council that the complaint about *Food for Thought* be upheld.

When I heard their conclusions I was sad, frustrated and angry. But not surprised.

If you buy advertising space you may find that your bill contains an extra payment to something called ASBOF. This is an organisation which collects money and funds the Advertising Standards Authority.

When I first protested about this deduction I was told that the deduction was compulsory and could not be avoided. However, I quickly found out that the deduction is entirely voluntary. The ASA is a voluntary body which has no statutory authority over you, me or anyone else.

I do not pay the ASBOF levy because I have absolutely no respect for the Advertising Standards Authority and do not see why I should help pay for it.

We currently have a simple policy as far as the ASA is concerned. We ignore them. We are happy that all the books which we publish are honest, legal, truthful and decent. We offer our readers a 'solid gold' guarantee which means that if they don't like a book they receive from us they can have their money back.

It is up to you what you do with your first letters from the ASA.

If your advertising is any good at all you are bound to receive complaints. First, there will be complaints from nutters who like to complain about anything and everything. Second, and most important, your competitors will complain about you in order to waste your time and to try and force you to spend money altering your advertising.

When you hear from the ASA you may feel that your options include hiring a lawyer, attempting to have a sensible correspondence with them or throwing their letters into the bin as soon as they arrive.

***

My experiences with MOPS, like those with the ASA, reminds me more of Kafka's book *The Trial* than anything else.

According to its own brochure the National Newspapers' Mail Order Protection Scheme was set up in 1975 to "formulate a Code of Practice and Regulations to ensure that the fast growing 'money off the page' mail order industry operated within well defined and controlled guidelines."

The stated purpose of MOPS is to "safeguard readers' money by reimbursing them should they lose money if the goods which have been ordered fail to be delivered as a result of an advertiser going into liquidation or bankruptcy or ceasing to trade. It also covers readers who have returned goods and not received a refund from a failed member advertiser." To join MOPS you have to fill in a collection of forms so complex that MOPS also sends out a letter explaining the application forms.

Mail order advertisers support MOPS by paying fees which vary according to the expenditure on advertising.

For example in the year 1997/8 the fees were as follows:

Advertising expenditure	Fee
£0-10,000	£200
£10,001-30,000	£400
£30,001-60,000	£740
£60,001-100,000	£1,300
£100,001-300,000	£2,250
£300,001-500,000	£3,350
£500,001-1,000,000	£5,500
£1,000,001-2,000,000	£6,000
£2,000,001-3,000,000	£6,500
£3,000,001-4,000,000	£7,000
£4,000,001-5,000,000	£7,500
£5,000,001 and above	£8,000

As far as we are concerned the most obvious injustice about all this is that we are expected to pay fees to MOPS on the assumption that we have paid rate card costs for our advertisements. Naturally, we buy most of them at considerably less than rate card.

For example, at the start of the 1998-9 MOPS year we paid a £200 fee for the right to buy £10,000 worth of mail order advertising in national newspapers. But although the first advertisement we bought (in *The Daily Telegraph*) cost us £3,000 the rate card value of the advertisement was £9,100. This meant that our £200 was virtually used up by that first advertisement. Effectively this meant that we had paid £3,200 for the advertisement (a 6.66% surcharge).

But we also feel that the bands discriminate against smaller advertisers. For example, an advertiser planning to spend £10,000 on advertising is expected to pay MOPS a fee of £200. An increase in rate card expenditure from between £100,001 and £300,000 to a level between £300,001 to £500,000 (a total of £199,999) would result in an additional fee of £1,100 whereas an increase in rate card expenditure from £4,000,000 to £5,000,000 would result in an additional fee of just £500.

We find it difficult to understand this. If it seems reasonable that an advertiser who spends more should pay a higher contribution towards MOPS why is the cost of being in MOPS cheaper for really big advertisers?

In 1997 I managed to obtain a copy of the financial statements for MOPS

I discovered that at the end of the previous financial year MOPS had around £2 million in cash and investments but that the organisation paid out only £15,726 in claims in the year ended 31.3.96. In the same period the organisation had staff costs of just under £200,000 and other operating costs of £304,960 and made a profit of £232,773. The MOPS explanation is that: "The existence of MOPS is not solely to pay claims but to undertake investigation of advertisers and the monitoring of their ongoing activities with a view to maintaining consumer confidence in payment with order advertising in national newspapers."

In 1997 we left MOPS but continued to buy some national newspaper advertising without being members of the organisation.

There were, however, some national newspapers which would not take our advertisements and so in April 1998 we decided to rejoin MOPS. Accordingly, we com-

THE TWO STAGE SELL

BRIGHT IDEA

Most off the page advertising relies upon the customer seeing the advertisement, being attracted by the offer, cutting out a coupon (or writing a short letter), writing a cheque, putting the coupon and the cheque into an envelope and posting both items off to the advertiser. If the advertiser takes orders by telephone this process can, of course, be made considerably easier.

However, some advertising relies on what is called a 'two stage sell'. Here what happens is that the advertisement which appears on the page in the newspaper or magazine merely invites readers to write in for more information or for a free brochure or booklet. The respondent may be required to pay a small charge towards the cost of postage and packing, though sometimes this charge may be allowed against any future purchase.

Naturally, the advertiser hopes that when the potential customer sees the brochure or booklet which they have been sent they will want to buy whatever it is that is being advertised. The big advantage to the advertiser is that in a brochure or booklet he can put far more information (and therefore sell his product that much more effectively) than he could possibly cram into an advertisement in a newspaper or magazine without buying acres of space and spending an absolute fortune.

One wonderful and underestimated advantage of the two stage sell is the fact that such advertisements are not monitored by MOPS and so you do not have to pay MOPS a levy on your advertising. If an advertisement is marginal this saving can be important and can make all the difference between success and failure.

pleted all the forms and answered a variety of questions.

Much to our astonishment we then received a demand for an additional £1,100. MOPS told us that according to their records we had exceeded the £300,001 limit in the year of 1996/7. We had, they said, spent £307,485. They therefore claimed an additional £1,100 in fees! MOPS did not send us a list of the advertisements we were supposed to have bought to substantiate this demand.

(You can see the effect of MOPS charging fees according to rate card expenditure when I tell you that our real total expenditure on advertising for that year – without VAT – was £172,254. And this sum included a good deal of magazine advertising which comes outside the scope of MOPS.)

We had no recollection of being asked for this payment in the past (and MOPS had certainly not chased us for the money) and so this came as rather a surprise.

We wrote back and pointed out that we were not aware that any sums were outstanding and that we were not aware of having spent over this band limit at rate card. We had, we pointed out, monitored our expenditure on advertising to make sure that this did not happen.

Furthermore, we pointed out that our advertising agency had told us that £15,000 of the alleged spend of £307,485 had consisted of advertisements which we had not paid for but which had been given to us free of charge. (If a newspaper fails to include a code or a correct address in an advertisement they will, quite sensibly, rerun the advertisement. But in addition to this our advertisements had on occasion been used as 'fillers' without our knowledge.)

With £15,000 worth of advertising deducted from the alleged expenditure of £307,485 we would clearly be well below the £300,001 threshold.

After MOPS had checked their records they told us that they had "not monitored" all the advertisements which had been given to us without charge and which we had listed as being part of the £15,000 worth of free advertising but effectively put an end to a protest which had, it seemed to us, been entirely reasonable by telling us that: "The fact that you did not incur any cost for these advertisements does not reduce the potential risk to the Scheme and the cover afforded by MOPS to readers."

In other words MOPS now seemed to be telling us that if a national newspaper chose to print an advertisement of ours without charge and without our permission we would still have to pay a commission to MOPS (an organisation which is run by the national newspapers!).

It seemed to us that this was totally outrageous. Technically, this meant that national newspapers could print, without our knowledge or permission, advertisements which had not worked and then charge us a commission through MOPS for this dubious privilege!

MOPS truly tries my patience.

If you wish to use national newspapers for your advertising, without joining MOPS, the easiest, and probably the best MOPS avoidance scheme is to use a two-stage sell.

Put an advertisement in a newspaper outlining the book you are selling and invite readers to write or telephone for details. Then send everyone who expresses an interest a brochure or leaflet describing your book. I understand that at the moment you do not have to be in MOPS to insert an advertisement of this type.

I have written at some length about these two organisations because if you begin publishing your own books you will almost certainly come up against these bodies.

None of the problems I have encountered in publishing have made me consider giving up publishing quite so much as trying to deal with the ASA and MOPS.

We have conquered the problems of finding printers and producing good looking, well made books at reasonable prices. We have conquered distribution and marketing problems. We publish honest, truthful and decent books. We give readers their money back if they do not like the book they buy. Our constant aim when writing and selling non fiction is to help give people more independence and knowledge. But, based on my personal experience, the ASA and MOPS are organisations which I would be perfectly happy to live without.

14. REVIEWS

Strictly speaking I suppose 'reviews' should be listed under the heading 'Free Advertising' but since a good deal of pompous nonsense is talked about book reviews I decided that reviews deserved a section of their own.

The first and most important thing to remember is that you should not expect your book to be widely reviewed. The chances are that if you publish it yourself then your book will be completely ignored – however good it is.

Newspapers and magazines which take books seriously enough to hire literary editors usually appoint vain, pseudo-intellectual nonentities who know virtually nothing about writing, books or publishing but who love going to literary parties and who bathe endlessly in their own (exclusively job derived) sense of self-importance.

Literary editors (most of whom would dearly love to write books but cannot)

DISAPPEARING BOOKS

If review copies constantly disappear – and literary editors ring up asking for replacements – then this can either be a good thing or a bad thing. It may be a good thing if the book disappears because everyone in the office takes it home to read. It may be a bad thing if someone in the office is selling the review copies to a local bookseller.

DON'T FORGET

show a natural aversion towards authors whose books sell in large quantities and much prefer to devote space to those authors whose books are unlikely to sell very well and whom they can, therefore, patronise endlessly.

My own experience is probably fairly commonplace: my first published books were widely reviewed in the national newspapers but the more successful I have become (and the more books I have sold) the rarer have become the reviews.

Most literary editors routinely dislike small, new publishing houses (and large, publishing houses which try to make a profit by producing books which there is a chance people might want to read).

Some literary editors proudly announce to anyone who will listen that they steadfastly and automatically refuse even to consider books published by small publishers. Literary editors much prefer to review books by academic authors who neither hope nor expect to make any money out of their books. They try to ensure that most of their space goes to publishing houses which have well established reputations but which have long since lost all touch with reality and which employ editors who prefer to be involved with esoteric volumes which may create some sort of mild, obscure and unthreatening academic controversy

The books which get most review space these days seem to me to be so unreadable and unwanted that everyone could save time by shipping them direct from the printers to the pulpers because not even the remainder merchants, who usually take unwanted, overstocks from publishing houses, want to buy them.

The literary editors, who decide which books get reviewed, reserve their great-

---

A CUTTINGS AGENCY

If you have high hopes that your book will be widely reviewed and quoted and you suspect that you may not see all the coverage then you should consider using a cuttings agency.

BRIGHT IDEA

This is not cheap but it will dramatically improve your chances of seeing cuttings relating to you or your book. Since cuttings agencies usually search on one particular word or name I suggest that rather than registering the title of your book you give your own name. This will ensure that you don't have to pay an additional sum whenever you have another book out.

To help ensure that your cuttings are accurately picked up by the agency's readers, make sure that you send them a copy of every press release you send out and details of every promotional activity you undertake.

It is common to be charged a fee based on the number of cuttings you are sent. This means that if a series of newspapers runs exactly the same review in all its editions, you will be charged for each individual cutting which is picked up – even if it duplicates a cutting you have already received.

est, most predictable and most intractable contempt for authors who publish their own books. One proudly announced that since I had started publishing my own work he would not dream of looking at (let alone reviewing) anything of mine that he was sent.

Literary editors who deliberately ignore self published books because they are self published have such a small knowledge of literature that they presumably do not know that many celebrated lions of literature have published their own books.

Literary editors sometimes seem to regard self publishing as cheating, as though the author, by ignoring or bypassing the traditional publishing route, was somehow producing a fake or making life too easy for himself. As far as literary editors are concerned it doesn't matter how good the book is, or how well it is bound, if it is self published it doesn't really count.

But despite the fact that reviews will probably be as rare as smiling traffic wardens you will still want to do everything you can to get reviewed.

Send out review copies at least 6 weeks before publication. (Unless you have written something so explosive that you need to keep it under wraps until publication date). You can enclose with your book a note asking for a copy of any review to be sent to you but this will almost certainly be ignored. If you want to save money you can send out a press release instead of a book – inviting literary editors to get in touch with you if they want a review copy. This will almost certainly result in silence.

You should compile your review list with some care. You may want to include national newspapers, (to say that getting a review in a national paper is something of a long shot is akin to saying that there may be rain in Britain at some time during the summer, but it will make you feel really good when or if it happens), large regional newspapers, specialist magazines and (if you are desperate for some sort of newspaper coverage) local newspapers.

If you know people working on newspapers it is usually considered part of the game to push your book onto them in the hope that they will give you a review. The London literary scene depends very much on this mutual back scratching among authors but since you and I will almost certainly be excluded from it (well, I am certainly excluded from it and I'm guessing that you will be too) we can look upon this inbred process with jaundiced, cynical and disapproving eyes.

As a self publisher you must, I fear, accept that your book will probably not be reviewed in the national press. This is neither rational nor fair but it is the way it is. If this makes you feel angry and frustrated then you can, perhaps, take some small comfort from the knowledge that most literary editors live entirely on borrowed power. The power they have comes with the job. When they lose their jobs (as most of them do every few years) they lose all their power.

15. THE IMPORTANCE OF THE FREE GIFT

You should remember that people usually need an inducement in order to persuade them to buy whatever it is that you are selling.

What do you give away with a book? Well, another book is one real possibility. Or a booklet, perhaps. If you have written a book about motorways in the north of England you could give away a booklet describing all the service stations on those motorways. If you have written a book about walking in the West Country you could give away a booklet listing the twenty best pubs in the region.

An inducement is a bribe to buy. It should, ideally, be something that seems to have even greater value than the product you are selling. It must be something that the reader really wants. If you can give your customers something free which is (or seems to be) worth more to them than the product they are buying then your product will become irresistible.

Your aim may be to spread your message and try to change the world but you won't be able to do either of those things unless you first of all grab people's attention. You can't do any good at all unless people listen to what you have to say.

16. NO RISK ORDERING: THE IMPORTANCE OF THE GUARANTEE

In order to persuade people to part with their money – and give you their custom – you have to remove as much of their risk as you possibly can. You have to take the risk – instead of your customer having to take it. The more you remove the risk involved in their doing business with you the more likely they will be to do business with you.

People are becoming increasingly distrusting and fearful and apprehensive about making a commitment to purchase anything – whether it be a product or a service. Most people have been disappointed. They have bought products which failed to do everything the advertisements claimed. They have been cheated.

Persuading complete strangers to send you their hard earned cash so that you, in turn, will send them a book requires a great deal of trust on their part. Most people have learnt to be cautious, sceptical and cynical about advertisement promises. How do they know that your book will be as good as you have made it sound? How do they know that you won't just send them a few pages of badly printed nonsense? How do they know that you will send them anything at all? How do they know that you won't just cash their cheque and run off with their money?

Your book may sound much better than anything else they have ever heard of. It may sound much more attractive and useful than anything that is likely to be available in the local book store. And because you can do business over the telephone or through the mail you are certainly much more convenient than any bookstore could ever be.

But, inevitably, at the back of everyone's mind will be the fear that you are maybe just trying to rip them off. Even if that isn't a fear they will undoubtedly worry that your book might not live up to expectations. There is a very good chance that every one of your potential customers will have, at some time or another, been cheated by someone. They may have been ripped off by another mail order company.

Of course, you don't want to rip them off. You are far more interested in a long term relationship with them than in making a small but immediate profit. You have made absolutely sure that the book you are offering lives up to all the promises in your advertisement. You are confident that when they see the book you are selling they will be pleased with it. You know that they will want to read it, keep it and, hopefully, recommend it to their friends. You believe that there is a good chance that they will be so pleased with the book you send them that they will order from you again, and become long term customers.

All your potential customers know that if they buy a book at a bookshop they can examine it carefully before they buy it. They can look at the contents list. They can read a few paragraphs at random if they want to. They can compare it with whatever else might be available. They can look at the quality of the paper and the binding.

But buying from you involves a risk.

And that risk may prevent them from ordering your book.

The simple answer is that in order to help them take the plunge and order your book you must remove all the risk from the transaction.

Somewhere in your advertisement you must make it perfectly clear that if, when they have received your book and had a chance to look at it, study it and read it, they do not feel that it was worth the money then you will give them their money back.

Simple!

With just a few words you have removed the risk from the transaction for the potential customer.

Three of the most powerful words in self publishing are 'Money Back Guarantee'.

Spell out exactly what you are promising to do (I suggest that you simply offer to refund the customer's money if, for any reason, he isn't happy with his purchase) and then make sure that you stick to your promise.

Publishing House offers a very simple and straightforward guarantee: if a purchaser of one of our books wants a refund then, as long as the book is returned within 28 days in saleable condition we return the customer's money. We make sure that refund cheques are sent out as a priority – customers who are unhappy for any reason don't have to wait for a month to get their money back. What could be simpler than that?

Removing the element of risk is particularly important if you are selling products by mail order – where the customer hasn't seen what you're selling and has to rely on your advertising literature. Providing a guarantee, and then sticking to it, is the best way I know of to build up a lifetime relationship with your customers.

By removing the risk you have immediately given yourself a massive advantage over ordinary publishers and high street bookshops.

Most of your potential purchasers know that if they buy a book from a bookshop they will have no chance at all of returning it for a refund if they subsequently discover that it isn't as good as they had hoped it would be.

But your guarantee means that they can even get their money back if they find another book they like better. They don't have to give a reason for returning the book and asking for a refund.

By promising your potential customers that if they don't like the product they buy from you then you will – without any fuss and without them having to explain why they don't like the book – give them a refund, you are immediately trumping all the advantages offered by the local neighbourhood bookshop.

Most important of all you are making it clear that you have total confidence in the book you are selling. And your confidence will be contagious.

We always draw attention to our guarantee because we think that removing the risk from the transaction is vital.

For example, on advertisements for my book called *Relief from Irritable Bowel Syndrome* we include the totally true phrase 'You have nothing to lose but your symptoms'.

The reader with IBS who sends us a cheque cannot lose. If the book is as good as we say it is then for just a few pounds he or she will have learnt how to deal with a life-disturbing problem. But if the book doesn't look good, and the advice doesn't sound convincing then the book can be sent back and a full refund obtained. There is no risk at all – but plenty of possible gain.

With a guarantee of this sort what sort of returns can you expect? Much less than you probably expect because most people will respond in an honest way. If you send them a book which they value they will be happy to keep it.

Most mail order publishers who offer a guarantee expect to receive about 5% returns. In other words five out of every 100 buyers will return the book they have bought and ask for their money back. If your product isn't as good as people expect it to be, or if your customers feel that they not received value for money, then you may get a much higher return rate than this. I know of one man in the mail order business who gave up and insisted that mail order operations were impossible after he consistently received between 60% and 70% returns.

(Having seen the book he was selling I am not surprised that his publishing venture failed.)

It is a good idea to keep an eye on the level of your returns because the number of returns you are getting will tell you how good a service, and product, you are providing. And if you want to be successful then you must provide a good service.

Mail order publishing really only works well if many of the people who buy one book from you go on to buy a second, a third, a fourth and so on.

17. RETURNS ARE A SELLING OPPORTUNITY

Try not to regard mail order returns as a hassle. Instead regard them as another selling opportunity. Send a cheque back within a day or two of getting the returned item and with the cheque enclose a letter of apology. It's also a good idea to enclose a voucher that can be used against some other item in your catalogue.

The customer who gets his refund quickly and painlessly will trust you. He or she now knows that your guarantee is as good as you say it is. He or she could become a good customer in the future.

And don't quibble about sending people their money back even if the book they are returning is in less than pristine condition. We have had books returned in a very dog-eared condition (obviously re-read many times), with pencil markings on the pages and food stains and cigarette burns on the cover. In theory we only offer to refund money to our customers if they send back a book in resaleable condition. But in practice we don't stick to that policy. Our aim is to keep our customers happy.

Of course, there always will be some people who will take advantage of your guarantee. There is absolutely no point at all in getting upset at these sad people. They have, through their own meanness, already carved out their own futures. They will spend their lives clipping out money off coupons and trying to persuade the check out girl at the local supermarket to cash them even though they haven't bought the item concerned.

Here are just a few of the more bizarre letters Publishing House has received from customers:

"I read and enjoyed this book very much. Would you please send me my money back now."

"I have read this book. Can I exchange it for another book."

"I have had my irritable bowel syndrome for twenty years. I tried your regime for two weeks but my symptoms have still not gone. I want a refund."

FASCINATING FACT

OUR RETURNS LEVEL

Since you are asking I will tell you that despite our solid gold guarantee our returns level runs at about 1% – and that includes customers writing in to say that their book has been damaged in the post, hasn't arrived at all or is not the book they ordered. (Sometimes they ordered the wrong book by mistake. Sometimes we sent them the wrong book. It doesn't matter whose fault it is we just send them the book they really want.) The bottom line is that we only refund cheques to less than 1 in 100 customers. It is one of the lowest return rates in the mail order business. I'm very proud of that.

"You should not charge for your books. They contain very valuable information which should be available to everyone free of charge."

(We wrote back to this complainant and pointed out that my books are available free of charge to everyone. All they have to do is visit their local public library. And if the library doesn't have the book in stock then they should simply ask the librarian to order it.)

18. DESPATCHING YOUR BOOKS

When you begin, and your publishing business is small, you can get away with buying a few sheets of stamps (the one organisation which will not give you any credit is the Post Office), an accurate set of parcel scales and a supply of padded bags. But if things go well it will not be long before you find that you need something more organised.

Publishing House is now big enough to be able to ignore stamps. Our outgoing mail is weighed, put into grey sacks, and collected daily by the Royal Mail which then takes appropriate sums from my bank account at regular intervals.

If we are doing a large scale mailshot we use a system called Mailsort. This means we sort the outgoing mail by post code entitling us to reduced rate postage. You need to send a minimum of 4,000 letters to use this system (or 1000 packets), and you will also need a computer program to sort the names and addresses into post code area. But, if you are planning regular, large mailings, the costs of setting up the system will soon be clawed back through the postage savings you will make. Once you get to the stage of doing mailings of this size it's probably worth asking for an appointment with a Royal Mail Business Services Representative. He or she will be able to guide you through all the services and savings available to you.

BRIGHT IDEA

PUTTING LEAFLETS IN WITH YOUR BOOKS

When you have published two or more books you can put a catalogue or leaflet describing and advertising your other publications. The more books you have on your back-list the more books you will be able to advertise when you send out books to your customers.

Mailing promotional material in this way costs you hardly anything. Unless you have a huge catalogue which weighs a great deal the chances are that your leaflet won't cost you anything in postage because it will be sent out free with a book you already have to post.

19. BUYING YOUR STATIONERY

When you begin you can simply obtain your stationery from a local stationery store. Easy. But when you start buying padded bags by the hundred (which you will do quite early on in your career as a publisher) you may find it easier to open an account with a supplier who will deliver to your door. You will almost certainly find it cheaper to buy stationery this way. (Although do be careful: the catalogues produced by mail order stationery companies are so inviting that it is very easy to order lots of things which look pretty and fun but which you do not really need.)

20. INSURANCE

If you work from home then you will need to make sure that you tell your insurance and mortgage company exactly what you are doing. And once you take delivery of your first batch of books you will have to start insuring your stock. And, of course, if you employ people to help you with your publishing operation you will need to make sure that they are insured. If you carry insurance then the chances are that nothing will ever happen. If you do not have any insurance then the chances are that someone hired to help you by carrying piles of books up and down the stairs will trip, fall and break a leg.

21. ORDERING REPRINTS

Ordering reprints has to be done well in advance. Printers are busier at some times of the year than at others. Ask your printer if he has any quiet times. You may be able to negotiate a special, low price if you can plan far enough ahead to be able to order your reprints at a time that is convenient to the printer. Unless paper prices have rocketed, or it is long time since your first printing, you will probably find that reprinted books cost you slightly less than copies of the original book you are reprinting. This should enable you to make a slightly higher profit.

22. SALES REPRESENTATIVES

Early in my career as a publisher I hired some freelance sales representatives to sell my books into the bookshops. This system works quite simply. Each salesman will work on behalf of a number of small or smallish publishing houses which cannot afford to hire their own sales representatives. When the salesman arrives at a bookshop he will talk about all the books his clients are currently trying to sell (including their backlists).

When I had sales representatives the arrangement I had was that the salesmen (and women) would receive a percentage of the sales made through the bookshops. However, I halted this arrangement quite early on in my career as a self publisher and do not, at the moment, use sales representatives.

I had no problem with the sales force (who, in my view, did remarkably well in view of the fact that bookshops are generally resistant to small publishing houses in general and self publishers in particular). The difficulty I did encounter was the fact that because I was spending quite a lot of money on newspaper and magazine advertisements, and also sending out quite a number of mailshots, I knew that a number of the bookshop orders that were generated were inspired by my advertisements. I knew that even without salesmen I would sell some books to bookshops (these would be usually on a 'firm sale' basis since the bookshops were invariably ordering only because they were responding to customers orders – if your advertisements are effective many of the people who see them will go into bookshops to order your books, even though you offer to send the book post free) but the problem was that it was impossible to differentiate between those orders which had been generated by the salesmen's visits to the bookshops and those which had been generated by my advertisements and mailshots. I knew that if I gave a commission to the salesmen on sales which had been triggered by my advertisements then I would soon be in trouble (since I was already paying for the advertisements!)

MARKETING IDEA

DISTRIBUTION DEALS

It is possible to arrange a distribution deal with an established, 'proper' publisher. You arrange to have your book set, printed and bound and then delivered to the 'proper' publisher. He will store and distribute your book with his own titles. Your book will be sold by his representatives and may even appear in his catalogue. You will be responsible for publicising and promoting your book. The snag, of course, is money. You will have to pay a handling charge of around 25% of the net receipts for this service. And since you will also have to pay anything between 35% and 65% to bookshops and wholesalers there will not be much left to cover your costs.

If you take this route you will have to watch out for returns from bookshops. If bookshops order and then later return vast quantities of your books you could still end up paying a commission on the original sale. Alternatively, you can arrange for your books to be handled by a trade distributor who will store your books and then make sure that bookshop orders are fulfilled. The snag is that you will be responsible for making sure that bookshops order your books!

23. STAFF

To begin with you may, if you have the time and the patience, be able to cope with everything that needs to be done yourself. But as your self publishing venture grows you will quickly find that you need help. This will, in part, be because there simply won't be enough hours in the day to put books into bags, deal with printers, bookshops and newspaper advertising departments, and get on with writing your next book. But it will also be because you will find that there are some aspects of publishing which you don't do as well (or enjoy as much) as the writing the books bit.

I am an incompetent administrator, a terrible bookkeeper, an awful accountant and utterly useless at running an office, dealing with real, live human beings, managing staff and doing many of the other things that a publisher has to do. My desk is always a total mess, I cannot remember what I did yesterday or what I am supposed to do tomorrow and if I add up a row of figures three times I get three different results. This happens even if I use a calculator. If I put a piece of paper down on my desk I can pretty well guarantee that it will be totally lost within a minute. My office is the land based equivalent of the Bermuda Triangle. (A little while ago I spent twenty minutes searching for two cheques. I then realised that I had put them into the shredder.)

Fortunately for me and my aspirations as a self publisher my friend and business partner Sue Ward is marvellous at all things practical. She understands and is a whizz at computers and can do things in Windows that make me back away in terror. She can get the best out of printers and print shops and people will work with her without walking out in despair (as would, I am sure, happen if I attempted to run Publishing House).

You, on the other hand, may find that you are good at doing everything and that all you need is a Girl or Man Friday to help you with the administrative chores and with packing books into padded bags.

24. SHOULD YOU CHARGE FOR POSTAGE AND PACKING?

Some mail order experts claim that people buying through the mail are blind to charges made for postage, packing and handling. You can, they say, add a postage, packing and handling charge of £2.95 or £3.95 onto the price of a book without losing a single sale.

My experience is different. We tested this hypothesis in the most scientific way we know how. We printed several thousand catalogues which were identical apart from the fact that half the catalogues offered books post free while the other half included a charge.

The result was very convincing. It seemed clear that the people who had received the catalogue with the extra charge for postage and packing were ordering fewer books than the people who had received the catalogue with books offered on a post free basis.

Since then we have not usually charged extra for postage and packing. (There are, of course, occasional exceptions. For example, if a book is particularly heavy then we may charge extra for postage. And if we are selling a book at a very low, giveaway price we may add a postage charge. We also charge extra for postage when sending books outside the UK.)

One advantage of charging extra for postage and packing is that if a customer returns an unwanted book then you only have to send back the price he paid for the book. You can keep the 'postage and packing' element of the price. Note that this only applies to unwanted (but perfect) books. If the book is damaged or faulty then you should refund the purchase price or replace the book (whichever the customer wants) *and* refund their postage costs.

25. YOU NEED AN ADDRESS WHERE ORDERS CAN BE SENT

Think very carefully about the address you are going to use. If you use your home address then the chances are that you will have readers calling in for tea. That might be very pleasant (depending, of course, upon the reader) but you will also find yourself receiving a good many other callers – and a good deal of uninvited mail. If you put advertisements in newspapers carrying your home address then you may find that you soon will not have any privacy left at all. And remember that if your publishing business grows so too will the mail and the number of callers.

There are two main alternatives to using your home address.

The first, which is by far the most expensive, is to rent or buy an office. I do not suggest you do this until your self publishing venture is an established success.

The second is to use some form of accommodation address. Your local Post Office will tell you how to rent a Post Office Box and this may, particularly to begin with, be the simplest and easiest solution. If you are expecting lots of different types of mail you can use more than one Post Office Box in order to help you differentiate between the types of mail.

26. HANDLING TELEPHONE CALLS

The telephone really becomes a problem when you start putting your telephone number on your advertisements. You should, therefore, think carefully before putting your home telephone number onto your advertisements. Do you really want people calling up 24 hours a day 7 days a week? The novelty might begin to fade after a week or two without sleep. You can, of course, have an additional line installed which you use exclusively for your publishing business. You can put a telephone answering machine onto the business line when you want to 'switch off'.

27. TAKING CREDIT CARD ORDERS

To begin with you can run your small publishing business by taking cheques or cash. But, if your business grows as I hope it will, then you will eventually find that customers want to know if you will also take credit cards.

The big snag with taking credit cards is that it means dealing with banks and banks are, of course, full of people who wear suits and regard fun and humour with the same sense of distaste most people reserve for septic tanks. Naturally, the fact that you will be dealing with banks means that there will be lots of reasons for charging you fees. There will, of course, be a joining fee and every time you take a credit card order you will have to pay a small but noticeable percentage of the gross price to the credit card company. The credit card service charge is likely to be 3.5% to 4.0% though some cards charge an even higher percentage. There will, inevitably, be a minimum annual service charge requirement so don't even think about taking credit cards unless you think your business is likely to be big enough.

The big advantage of taking credit cards is that you will be able to take telephone orders for your books. Research by mail order companies has shown that advertisements do considerably better (and I really do mean considerably better) if customers can order by telephone as well as through the mail. Put a telephone number on an advertisement and tell your potential customers that you will accept payments by credit card and you could easily increase the number of orders you take by a half. That is enough to turn many loss making advertisements into profitable advertisements.

28. DEALING WITH QUERIES

A surprisingly large amount of your time will be taken up with queries. Some of these will be serious, some will be trivial and some will be quite unbelievable. You will receive letters from people wanting you to publish their book. You will receive letters from people wanting free copies of your book. (Unless you're in a good mood and feeling generous tell them that your book is available free of charge through every public library.) You will receive letters complaining about something you said or didn't say. You will receive letters offering you unique business opportunities. You may find that life will be easier if you have some cards or letters printed with appropriate messages already printed on them. You could either have several versions, all containing different messages, or one version with several messages listed – allowing you to tick the most appropriate response.

At Publishing House we use as many pre-printed letters as we can, and the queries are pre-sorted into query types so that, theoretically, anyone can deal with them. After years of research we have come up with the following categories of problems which seem to crop up most often:

1. **No Address**: when the customer sends an order and payment but no address.
2. **No Cheque**: when the customer sends in an order but no payment
3. **No Signature**: when the customer sends an order and unsigned cheque
4. **What Book**: when the customer doesn't specify what they want to order
5. **Wrong Date**: when the customer wrongly dates their cheque
6. **Credit Card**: when the customer provides incorrect card details

For all the above you will need to contact the customer (for "no address" customers we always write via their bank but you will probably have no way of contacting customers who send postal orders). Once this has been done we move the paperwork to a 'pending' file for each category of query while we wait for the customer to contact us. Sometimes the customer will never get in touch again – even when you have written a couple of times – and so we have a large box of unresolved queries going back several years.

7. **Refunds**: when the customer wants their money back.

Refunds should be dealt with quickly – the customer may still want to buy from you again. Keep a note of the date you make the refund and the cheque number.

8. **Exchanges**: when the customer wants to swop one book for another.

This is usually because the subject matter of the first book is not suitable, but it could be because you sent out the wrong book in the first place. We are usually happy to exchange books, but make sure you keep an eye on the customer's history with you. We had one lady who kept sending books back (which had clearly been read) saying they were unsuitable and so could she have something else. In the end we had to suggest that she use the library instead of us!

9. **Damaged/Lost in Post**: when the customer does not receive his or her book, or receives it in a damaged condition

If the book is damaged then you should immediately offer a refund or replacement. If it is lost then send a replacement by first class post (check that you have the correct address details for the customer). In both instances you should be able to claim against the Royal Mail for your loss. To make a claim you may be required to prove that you posted the goods in the first place. The computer programme we use keeps a 'posting report' which logs every item we send out and the Royal Mail accept this as our proof of posting.

10. Bounced Cheques

Your bank will advise you if this happens and then it's up to you to contact the customer to get your money. You may prefer to wait until a customer's cheque has cleared before you send anything to them – particularly if your book is sold at a high price. We get such a high number of orders each day that it would be an administrative nightmare to clear each cheque before processing the order so we take the risk. Luckily, only a small number of cheques bounce.

11. Cheques Cashed in Error

Sometimes we cash a cheque and then, when it comes to processing the order, realise the customer has not sent their address. We then have to wait and hope the customer eventually contacts us to see where their book is. It doesn't happen often.

12. Delete From Mailing List
13. Catalogue Requests
14. Forward Orders: when a customer asks us to despatch on a particular date or sends a postdated cheque

Our trade sales to bookshops, wholesalers and library suppliers are dealt with separately and not mixed in with private customers. This means that when we select names for a direct customer mailing (say customers who have bought *Food for Thought*) we do not select bookshop names by mistake.

29. PACKING BOOKS

You can, if you like, try packing up books with brown paper, string, padding and sealing wax. But I strongly recommend that you use padded bags of some kind. A padded bag will provide all the protection your book needs to get it through the post safely. Make

---

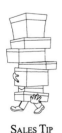

SALES TIP

POSTING ABROAD

You should obtain copies of all the Post Office leaflets which describe how to send parcels, packets and letters abroad. As far as postage is concerned we regard the world as consisting of three areas: UK, Europe and the rest of the world. We usually send books within the UK without any extra charge for postage or packing. We charge a small sum for postage and packing within the rest of Europe. And we charge slightly more for postage and packing to the rest of the world. We never aim to make money out of postage charges.

sure that you choose a light padded bag otherwise you will end up paying out a lot of extra money on postage. Books are heavy enough by themselves. You want your books to arrive at their destination in perfect condition but you also want the bag to be as light as possible. Also, try to use self-seal bags or you will spend ages using sticky tape, staples or string.

Unless you plan to take all your packaged orders to the Post Office to be stamped you will need a set of scales to weigh each parcel. We managed like this for quite a while but now we have a heavy-duty machine which can weigh full sacks of mail.

BOOKS AND BAGS

When choosing a size for your book bear in mind the fact that it will have to fit inside a padded bag. Check out the sizes of padded bags before insisting on having your book published in a very unusual size. If you can't pack and mail your oddly sized book without using cardboard, sealing wax and string you may regret your impetuosity and determination to be different.

SALES TIP

---

30. PROCESSING ORDERS

If computers frighten you then you can, to begin with, keep your orders in a large notebook. You can use the same notebook to help you keep details of the money you have received. But if your business grows then you will obviously need to set up a computer programme to keep details of your customers. You may, if you are clever with computers, be able to set up your own programme. But don't worry if you aren't clever with computers. You can always buy a programme designed for mail order. The big advantage of a purpose-built programme is that it will be ready programmed to give you much of, if not all, the information you are likely to need.

I would suggest that it is almost certainly worthwhile investing in a professionally-produced programme. We at Publishing House have tried two software programmes and the one we use at the moment certainly makes life much easier. It enables us to keep details of all our customers, what they have ordered and when, how they paid, where they saw the book advertised, when we sent out the order and any other general notes we want to keep.

Remember that if you keep records on a computer you will have to register your database under the Data Protection Act.

SALES TIP

AN APOLOGY

If, for any reason, you cannot deliver an ordered book within the promised time you should write and explain in honest, accurate detail what has gone wrong and why you cannot fulfil your promise. If a supplier has let you down then explain why and how – and describe what you normally do to make sure that this doesn't happen. If all your book stock has been destroyed in a fire then say so – and explain why and how the fire started and what you are doing about it. Remember how annoying it is when you are stuck on a train or at an airport and no one bothers to tell you why there is a delay. Finally, offer to send the reader his or her money back.

31. KEEPING TRACK OF WHERE THE ORDERS HAVE COME FROM

It is absolutely vital that you keep track of where your orders come from. You must know whether an advertisement or a mailshot has worked because if you don't then you may waste a great deal of money repeating an ineffective advertisement or lose a great deal of money by failing to repeat an effective advertisement.

If you use a computer then it isn't difficult to devise a simple spreadsheet to help you keep count of the orders received from individual advertisements. And by putting into the spreadsheet the cost of the advertisement and the cost of fulfilling those orders you can see at any instant (and at the end of every day) whether or not you are making a profit. If you use specially-produced computer software then it should include all the programmes you need to track orders automatically.

BRIGHT IDEA

SAFETY FIRST

Whether you keep your customers' names and addresses on bits of paper or in a computer make sure that you keep at least one constantly updated copy somewhere safe. If there is a fire you can replace equipment but your database of names and addresses is irreplaceable and potentially extremely valuable. We make a complete back up copy every single day which is taken out of the office at night. As a further precaution a second weekly copy is made and stored away from the office.

32. KEEPING THE ACCOUNTS

If you are as hopeless as I am at doing accounts (I resent time spent poring over receipts and even the simplest accounts software package is a mystery to me) you will probably want to appoint an accountant if you don't already have one. Ask around your friends to find an accountant who seems trustworthy, honest and reasonably priced.

You must remember that if your publishing venture does well and your turnover reaches a certain level (this varies from time to time according to the whims of the Chancellor of the Exchequer) you will have to register for Valued Added Tax (VAT). This isn't necessarily the disaster it might sound for when you are VAT registered you will be able to claim back the VAT you have paid on goods and services which you needed to buy to be able to publish your book. At the time of writing there is no VAT on books so you won't have to claim any VAT from the people who buy your books. Unless you have any other income which is liable to VAT (if, for example, you are paid for writing newspaper articles or columns or you have books which are published by conventional publishers) you will probably find that filling in the quarterly VAT form brings you a nice cheque from Her Majesty's Customs and Excise department.

33. CUSTOMER CARE

If you want your venture into publishing to succeed then you must look after your customers. Your aim should be not to think of ways to make life easier for you but to think of ways to make life easier and better for them. You want your customers to be satisfied so that they come back again and again to buy your books. You also want them to be so happy with the service you provide that they give your name to their friends. Providing a good service and a simple guarantee isn't enough. If you establish a good relationship with your customers then they will want you to grow and succeed (though not so much that you lose your friendliness and stop giving a good, personal service).

The rarest commodities in our world are honesty, respect and integrity and I believe that people do respect these old fashioned virtues. The best way to grow stronger is to delight your customers so much that they help spread the word about your book(s) by word of mouth. Nothing sells books (or, indeed, anything else) as effectively as word of mouth advertising.

Conventional publishers have one absolutely enormous drawback: their only contact with their customers is through a third party (the bookshops which sell their books). Naturally this makes it difficult for a conventional publisher to build up any sort of relationship with his customers. It is, indeed, virtually impossible for a publisher even to know who his customers are under those circumstances.

Having the names and addresses of your customers on a computer database

SMALL AND FRIENDLY

CUSTOMER CARE

One of the big advantages you have over the conglomerates is that yours is a small and friendly business whereas they run large, impersonal empires. People tend to like small and friendly and dislike large and impersonal so use your advantage to the full. Printing in vast quantities means that they will be able to beat you on price but you can definitely beat them on service and quality.

You should always send out a short friendly note with every order (it doesn't have to be handwritten or even signed) to thank the customer for ordering from you.

But there is something else you can do to establish your friendly image. Once you have built up your business you will probably produce a catalogue and this will offer you a great opportunity to build a relationship with your customers. You can include all sorts of information emphasising the friendliness of your company, and you can introduce yourself (and your staff) to your customers.

Here, for example, is a "Who We Are" section from one of the Publishing House catalogues:

<u>*Who We Are - And What We Do*</u>

John Fryer is in charge of the mighty computer and will process your order through the system. We think he is lucky because he can always blame the computer when things go wrong, but the rest of us have to take the blame ourselves! (Only joking, John). If your book gets lost in the post John will send out a replacement for you immediately. And if, for any reason, you want to send a book back for a refund (though we can't imagine why you would want to do that) then John will arrange for a cheque or card credit refund to be sent out to you.

Jean Woolley is in charge of our Customer Service Department and is that special person without whom the office would grind to a halt. She opens hundreds of envelopes every day, sorts out all the cheques and generally makes sure that everyone else can do their job. If you have any special requests in connection with your order please drop her a line or give her a ring. She will arrange for gift cards and letters to be sent out with presents. Jean is also the person who will write to you if you forget to sign your cheque! We all like Jean a lot, <u>and</u> she makes a wonderful cup of tea!

Faye Stockwell is the latest recruit to join the team at Publishing House. Faye is in charge of our marketing department and also helps out with general book production.

Sue Ward is the Publishing Director and likes to think she oversees the whole operation here at Publishing House. Of course, she really just sits in her office all day drinking tea while the rest of the team get on with the real work. She has been known to edit the occasional book and design a few advertisements now and then.

means that you can write to your customers on a regular (or irregular) basis to tell them about new books you are publishing or to offer them special deals on books that they already know about.

From time to time it is well worthwhile asking yourself why your current customers originally bought from you – and why they are likely to buy from you now. What is the undervalued (and possibly unstated) benefit to your customers of doing business with you?

For example, my monthly Health Letter is, superficially, a source of independent medical advice and information. But it is, I hope, a good deal more than that. I aim to remove some of the fear and anxiety that is these days associated with health and health care. I also try to provide my readers with a companion who can guide them to a knowledge and understanding of better health and improved health care, and give them an ability to deal knowledgably with health care professionals (whether they be orthodox or complementary practitioners) and a feeling that they are not alone in a world where loneliness is endemic.

34. DEVELOP YOUR BACKLIST

In the good old days publishers used to pay a great deal of attention to their backlist catalogue. A publisher's aim would be to find authors who would, over the years, write a number of steadily selling books. Promoting a new book by an author would, therefore, bring in new readers to buy and read his previous books. A good backlist catalogue could turn a marginally profitable publishing house into a relatively successful venture.

Most of today's modern publishers seem far too busy searching for this season's blockbuster success to take much interest in developing a good catalogue of backlist titles.

You, on the other hand, should take great care of your backlist. As you publish more and more new books you should take care to continue to sell the old books.

You should automatically include a copy of your backlist catalogue with every book you send out.

MARKETING IDEA

PRE-PUBLICATION DISCOUNTS

Try offering your book at a discounted price to readers who order before publication. Try something like this: "After January 1st next year this book will sell in bookshops for £19.95. But if your order is received by December 31st you will save £5 on the published price and receive your book for £14.95. Put your order and cheque in the post today."

35. SELLING A BOOK IS THE BEGINNING — NOT THE END

Selling a product or a service to a new customer should always be a beginning and not an end. It is in your interests to make sure that your customers know how to get the best out of whatever it is that you are selling. If your business is not doing well then the chances are that you are either not providing what your customers (or potential customers) really want or someone else is providing a better product or service or the same product or service at a more competitive price.

Your customers should think of you as a friend. You should work with and for your customers. It is far more profitable in the long run. You may be able to make short term money by ripping people off. But if you want to create something worthwhile then you must encourage your customers to trust you. Provide good service (defined as high quality goods, provided in the right quantity and with a good spirit) and when things go wrong (as they assuredly will, even though you may do your best to avoid and anticipate problems) apologise and put things right in a good spirit too. If something does go badly wrong try to re-establish your fractured relationship with the customer by giving him or her a free gift. Try to deliver more than you promise. You should certainly never deliver less than you promise.

Remember that honesty and decency do lead to long term success – even though, in the short term, they may prove expensive and seem counter-productive. People do respect honesty and integrity.

Part Six

Increase Your Profits

(and make even more money)

"No profit grows where is no pleasure taken"
WILLIAM SHAKESPEARE

1. SERIAL RIGHTS

For reasons which I do not even begin to understand newspapers will pay far more when they are buying the right to serialise or take extracts from a book than they will if they are buying an article or a series of articles. They will pay thousands of pounds for an extract from a book when they would have probably paid only hundreds of pounds for an identical article.

I've sold serial rights in scores of books and I've written (literally) thousands of articles and columns for newspapers and magazines and I honestly have no idea at all why tough newspaper editors who will complain bitterly about a feature writer's £5 taxi bill on an expenses claim will happily authorise cheques for thousands of pounds (dollars or whatever) when bidding for the right to print something from a book.

A good friend of mine once wrote an article about the royal family. He then offered the article to a number of newspaper and magazine editors. One editor was mildly interested and offered £300 for the piece. The other editors either sent the article back or ignored it completely.

My friend (I'll call him Jack though that isn't his name) thought that the piece was worth considerably more than £300 but he wasn't exactly in a strong position. He either accepted the £300 he had been offered or kept the article and got absolutely nothing for it.

"Why don't you turn it into a book?" another writer asked him.

"A book!" said Jack, clearly horrified. "I've never written a book. Besides the article is only 3,000 words long and I really don't think I could stretch it much further."

"You don't have to stretch it," the other writer told him. "But instead of offering it as an article offer it as an extract from a forthcoming book. Think up a sexy title, write a short foreword, an introduction and a contents list and call your 3,000 word article Chapter One. Then get someone with a colour printer to design and print out a dummy cover for you."

"Once you've done that get a couple of dozen copies of everything made, put them into folders and send them off to the editors who you think might be interested."

Now, newspaper editors don't want to have to go to the trouble of reading a whole book. (To be perfectly honest, after working for just about every paper in what used to be known as Fleet Street, I'm not entirely sure that there are many newspaper editors around who actually could read a book.) They don't want to have to plough through several hundred pages of text in order to find a few thousand words they can use in their paper. Editors want to be presented with a nice, neat package ready for publication.

Jack followed his friend's advice and sold his article (now redefined as a book extract) within five days. Three editors telephoned with offers and Jack finally did a deal for £8,500. Since he was selling an extract from a forthcoming book he sold only first British serial rights. Naturally, this meant that he could then also sell foreign rights to newspapers and magazines around the rest of the world.

I have told this tale to illustrate the point that book extracts do command a higher price than ordinary articles.

If you decide to try and sell serial rights to newspapers and/or magazines you should offer your book to any publications which you think could be interested.

National newspapers will almost certainly offer the biggest sums but do not forget that regional and local papers may also be interested in taking an extract if your book is likely to be of interest to their readers.

Valuable Tips When Selling Serial Rights

1. When selling anything to a newspaper watch out for the infamous clause 'payable on publication'. Do not accept a contract or commissioning letter containing this phrase or anything like it. Your contract or letter should make it clear that the newspaper is agreeing to pay the sum agreed for whatever rights you are selling. If the phrase 'payable on publication' appears then you will not get paid if, for any reason, your book extract or article does not appear. Newspapers and magazines are notorious for buying material which they never use. The phrase 'payable on publication' gives them a wonderful let out and enables them to avoid paying you if a member of the royal family breaks a limb and all the commissioned material is suddenly thrown out of the paper. It is disappointing enough not to see your piece in print. Not getting paid makes the whole sorry business even more painful – particularly since it is extremely likely that the other editors who were interested in and excited by your book or article will, by now, have lost all interest in it. Newspaper editors have the attention span of five year old children and lose interest in features and stories very quickly.

2. I only ever sell local serial rights and you should too. Never, ever part with copyright in anything. Whether you are selling a book extract, serial rights, an article or a column you should only sell first local serial rights. If you are selling an article to a British paper then you should sell them First British Serial Rights. This gives the publication the 'first' right to publish the material. If you have already sold the article to one paper and you are now selling subsequent rights then these can be described as Second

British Serial Rights, Third British Serial Rights and so on. Or you could simply sell the right to publish the material once. When you have sold your book about tennis to a national newspaper you can try selling additional rights to a specialist sports magazine.

3. Ask (or insist) that the editor put the words 'Copyright Vernon Coleman 1998' at the bottom of your article or book extract. If you don't want to give your copyright to me then you can insert your own name (and the correct year) in the appropriate places. If the article is taken from or is (however loosely) associated with a book you have written then make sure that you ask the editor to make sure that the copyright notice is accompanied by the name of the publishing house, the price and, if appropriate, the date of publication.

4. It is your responsibility to make sure that your article or book extract contains nothing libellous. In the good old days publishers and editors used to stand by their authors and writers. These days I am afraid that you have to assume that you are going to be on your own. If the paper which has published your work is sued then there is a good chance that they will do whatever protects their own interests while throwing you to the dogs. It is not uncommon for newspapers to settle with people taking libel action against them. This can make it extremely difficult for the freelance writer to formulate any sort of defence. Worse still, it is not unknown for a newspaper which has settled out of court to then demand that the writer pay their costs and whatever damages they paid.

5. Ask the editor to make sure that his newspaper's syndication department knows that the article is your copyright and that any enquiries from other editors wanting to publish your piece should be passed on to you.

6. If you are selling serial rights from a book which you have published, and which definitely exists, you should ask the editor to allow you to sell your book 'off the page'. All this means is that at the bottom of the extract which appears in the paper something like this will appear: "Readers can buy a copy of Vernon Coleman's book direct from the publishers and save £X off the published price. To obtain your copy send your name and address and a cheque or postal order for £Y (cheques should be made payable to Publishing House) to: Vernon Coleman Book Offer, Publishing House, Trinity Place, Barnstaple, Devon EX32 9HJ."

2. FOREIGN RIGHTS

In an attempt to find an American distributor for our books I went to the London Book Fair. I also wanted to have a look around to see what the 'big boys' were doing. While

I was there I was rather depressed. Everywhere I looked publishers seemed to be doing exactly the same things. There was a 'follow the leader' air to the whole dismal business. I remembered why I had lost faith and interest in traditional publishing companies, and had been happy to start publishing my own books.

When I left the book fair, which was held in Olympia, I walked back to Paddington Station to catch the train, through Kensington Gardens. By the time I had reached the station I had cheered up. I had realised that the fact that most big publishing companies are still playing 'follow the leader' (without really knowing who the leader is, or where they are heading) is excellent news for a small, innovative and daring publishing company.

The fact is that there is a world wide market for books which are different and which are written with passion. We have books on sale all around the world and rarely a week goes by without our receiving a letter, fax or telephone call from a foreign publisher wanting to publish one of our books.

FINANCIAL TIP

INDIAN CHARITY

At various points in your publishing career you will almost certainly receive requests from people in India for copies of you book. They will promise untold riches and have great plans for selling your book to millions of their countrymen. Sadly, none of this is likely to come true. Regard sending book samples to India as a form of charity.

---

3. MULTIMEDIA

As a self publisher you should be enormously grateful for the opportunities offered by 'multimedia'. Tapes, CDs, software and the Internet have promised so much for so long that just about all the big publishers now spend a great deal of their time and money on attempting to market products in this area.

Sadly, for them but not for you and I, they have not found the multimedia explosion to be as profitable as it is fashionable. While the big publishing companies concentrate more and more of their money and energies on multimedia opportunities you and I can carry on with selling books and making a profit.

I have some personal experience of the multimedia fashion in publishing. I began selling computer software versions of my books back in 1981 and the remainder of the

CONTRACTS FOR FOREIGN SALES

Foreign publishers who have heard about or seen one of our books and want to publish it in their country will ask us to send them a contract. Here is a copy of one of the contracts we routinely use. If you use an agent then they should provide the contracts for you.

MEMORANDUM OF AGREEMENT made this day the 27th February 1998

BETWEEN

VERNON COLEMAN, PUBLISHING HOUSE, TRINITY PLACE, BARNSTAPLE, DEVON EX32 9HJ, ENGLAND ("the Proprietor")

AND

OR AM PUBLISHING HOUSE LTD., 28 YITZCHAK SADEH STREET, TEL AVIV, ISRAEL
("the Publisher") of the other part

AND

I PIKARSKI LTD., LITERARY AGENCY, PO BOX 4006, TEL AVIV, ISRAEL
("the Agent") of the other part

WHEREAS

The Proprietor has agreed to grant the Publisher a license to publish in the HEBREW language ("the contracted language") on the terms hereinafter set out an original work entitled:

BODYPOWER by Vernon Coleman
("the Work")

IT IS MUTUALLY AGREED:

1.   (a)   In consideration of the payments hereinafter mentioned and subject to the provisions of this Agreement hereinafter contained, the Proprietor hereby grants the Publisher an exclusive license for the term of this Agreement (subject to earlier termination as hereinafter set out) to print, reprint, publish and sell an edition ("the Publisher's Edition") of the Work in the contracted language throughout the world to and for resale to the book trade and by no other means and to no other market; electronic, optical and digital rights are specifically excluded from this Agreement.

        (b)   The Publisher shall have the right for the purpose of promoting the Publisher's Edition to use or authorize the use of short extracts and illustrations from the Publisher's Edition in such manner and by such media as the Publisher may consider advisable, subject to the proviso that the Proprietor's name (Vernon Coleman) accompanies any such extract from the said Work as the author of the completed said Work. The license granted to the Publishers in Clause 1 hereof does not cover any illustrations included in the work and the Publishers must make their own arrangements with the owners of such illustrations for the right to include the illustrations in their editions.

        (c)   The license and rights hereby granted are personal to the Publisher and may not be assigned or sub-licensed without the Proprietor's prior consent in writing, nor may the Publisher's Edition be published under any imprint other than the Publisher's.

        (d)   All rights in the Work apart from the license and rights granted thereunder are expressly reserved by the Proprietor.

2.   The term of this grant is for a period of seven years from the date of this agreement, at which time all rights herein granted shall automatically revert to the Proprietor.

3.   The Proprietor undertakes and agrees:

        to supply the Publisher free of charge with three sets of the final typescript or printed copy of the Work; and

4. The Publisher undertakes and agrees:

(a) that the Publisher's Edition will contain a true and accurate translation of the text of the Work procured at the Publisher's own expense and that no text or authorized illustrations from the Work will be altered or omitted from the Publisher's Edition, nor any additional material included, without the prior consent in writing of the Proprietor;

(b) that where the source of any material reproduced in the Proprietor's Edition from the Work has been credited in the Work, it will be similarly credited in the Publisher's Edition;

(c) that unless otherwise agreed the Publisher's Edition will be similar in format, size and paper and binding quality to the Work (but that subject to this provision the preparation, publication, distribution, price and promotion of the Publisher's Edition shall be within the discretion of the Publisher); the Publisher may only edit and add materials to the extent mandatory to achieve a competent and idiomatic translation. Such editions and revisions shall not materially change the meaning or otherwise materially alter the text;

(d) that each copy of the Publisher's Edition will contain a notice in English and Hebrew stating the following: "Copyright 199_ by Vernon Coleman"

(e) that the Publisher will publish the Publisher's Edition by not later than eighteen (18) months from date of this contract.

(f) that the first printing of the Publisher's Edition will consist of not less than 1,000 copies.   *S. S*

(g) that the Publisher will keep the Proprietor informed through the intermediary of the Agent of the quantities of each reprinting of the Publisher's Edition;

(h) that prior to the publication of the Publisher's Edition the Publisher through the Agent will notify the Proprietor of the price at which each copy of the Publisher's Edition will be sold in each country in which it will be sold ("the Published Price") and will from time to time keep the Proprietor informed of any changes in such Published Price;

(i) that within thirty days (30) of the publication of the Publisher's Edition, the Publisher will furnish the Proprietor with six (6) copies,

j) that the Publisher through the Agent will take such steps as may be reasonably required by the Proprietor to secure and protect the Proprietor's rights in each of the countries in which the Publisher's Edition may be published;

(k) that the Publisher will take all reasonable steps to promote the sale of the Publisher's Edition;

(l) that forthwith on the Publisher's Edition going out of print or off the market the Publisher will notify the Proprietor accordingly in writing (and for the purpose of this Agreement the Publisher's Edition shall be deemed to be out of print or off the market if the number of copies thereof in the possession or under the control of the Publisher shall be less than 250 copies).

5. (a) The Publisher shall pay to the Agent for transmission to the Proprietor a non-refundable advance of US$ 500 [United States dollars five hundred] on account and in anticipation of the royalties specified in Clause 6 hereof such advance to be payable on signature of this Agreement by the Publisher.

(b) If the amount payable on the date of the signing of this Agreement under sub-clause (a) of this Clause 5 is not paid, then Clause 1 and 3 hereof notwithstanding and without prejudice to such other rights as the Proprietor may have under this Agreement the Publisher shall have no license or rights in respect of the Work and the Proprietor shall not be obliged to supply the copies of the Work or film as herein before provided for.

(c) If payment is not received within 30 days after executed signatures, the Publisher shall pay 1.5%

♦ If you are using illustrations or photographs provided by someone else then you will need to amend your contract accordingly per month on the amount due.

6.   Subject to Clause 10 hereof, the Agent on behalf of the Publisher shall pay to the Proprietor a royalty on every copy of the Publisher's Edition sold by the Publisher as follows:

An amount equivalent to 6% [six percent] of the retail price on the first 3,000 copies, 8% [eight percent] of the retail price on the next 3,000 copies and 10% [ten percent] of the retail price on all copies thereafter sold in each country in which the publisher's Edition is sold.

7.   (a)   The Publisher shall keep accurate accounts and records (together with all supporting vouchers) in respect of its printing and sales of the Publisher's Edition and on all matters relevant to the calculation of royalties under this Agreement and shall if so required make such records, accounts and vouchers available to the Proprietor or its authorized representatives.

(b)   The Publisher shall deliver to the Proprietor through the Agent within 60 days of each six monthly period ending on the 30th of June and 31st of December in each year a statement certified by the Publisher's auditors reflecting all sales, published price(s) and other information relevant to the calculation of royalties under this Agreement in respect to such a period. Such statement shall also reflect the number of unsold copies of the Publisher's Edition in the possession of or under the control of the Publisher at the end of such a period. The Publisher shall at the time of delivery of each such statement pay to the Proprietor through the Agent the royalties due thereunder.

(c)   Payment for royalty statements are due 60 days after the 30th of June and the 31st of December. If payment is not received within 30 days from those dates, the Publisher shall pay an additional amount equivalent to 1.5% per month on the amount due per title.

8.   All sums of money payable to the Proprietor under this Agreement shall be paid to the Agent in United States of America dollars without any deduction (other than deductions of tax which the Publisher may be obliged by law to make) in respect to bank charges or otherwise. If the Publisher shall make any such tax deduction it shall at the time of delivery of the relevant statement under Clause 7(b) supply the Proprietor with a certificate from the relevant tax authority of the tax so deducted.

9.   No extension of time or other indulgence which may be granted by the Proprietor to the Publisher shall constitute a waiver of the Proprietor's strict rights under this Agreement.

10.   No copies of the Publisher's Edition shall be sold by way of remainder within a period of three years of the date of first publication by the Publisher. For the purpose of the Agreement the term "remainder" shall be deemed a sale at less than two-thirds of the Published Price originally notified to the Proprietor. If the Publisher shall wish to remainder any copies after the period of three years aforesaid it shall first give the Proprietor a reasonable opportunity to buy the same at the proposed remainder price. Notwithstanding Clause 6 hereof, no royalty shall be payable in respect of any sale to the Proprietor thereunder, or in respect of any sale at less than the Publisher's cost price of such a copy.

11.   Without prejudice to any claim which the Proprietor may have against the Publisher for damages and/ or otherwise, the Proprietor may forthwith by summary notice terminate this Agreement in any one or more of the following circumstances:

(a)   If the Publisher shall fail to make any payment on its due date as required by this Agreement or within seven days thereafter;

(b)   If the Publisher (being a company) shall go into liquidation (other than a bona fide liquidation for the purpose of reconstruction the terms of which have been notified to the Proprietor prior to such a liquidation) or shall suffer a Receiver to be appointed in respect of any part of its undertaking or (being an individual or partnership) such Publisher or any partner thereof shall become bankrupt;

(c)   If the Publisher shall commit any other breach of this Agreement which, in the case of a breach capable of remedy, it shall fail to remedy within thirty days of receiving written notice from the Proprietor requiring it to do so;

♦ Remember that you may have to pay tax in the country where the book is being published. Tell the tax authorities here if this happens and you may be able to avoid being "double-taxed".

(d)   If the Publisher shall allow the Publisher's Edition to remain out of print or off the market (as defined in paragraph 1 of Clause 4 hereof) for more than six months;

(e)   If the Publisher shall sell any copies of the Publisher's Edition by way of remainder.

12.   On termination of this Agreement, howsoever arising:

(a)   The license and all rights granted to the Publisher thereunder shall forthwith cease with the proviso that if and only if such termination shall not have arisen under the provisions of Clause 11 hereof, the Publisher may, for a period of six months from such date of termination and subject to the payment of royalties as provided for in Clause 6 hereof dispose of any copies of the Publishers Edition already printed as at the date of termination, by the means to the markets set out in Clause 1 (a) hereof;

(b)   The Publisher agrees that upon the expiration of the present contract it will not use the Hebrew translation in any other work, including works compiled by itself, without prior permission in writing from the Proprietor;

(c)   All moneys which may be owing by the Publisher to the Proprietor under this Agreement shall be due and payable immediately; and

(d)   The Publisher shall at the option of the Proprietor either destroy or hand over to the Proprietor all film, printing plates and other materials produced for the Publisher's Edition.

13.   Any notice required to be given by either part under this Agreement shall be in writing and shall either be delivered by hand or by registered first class airmail to the other party at the address set out above or at any other address subsequently notified.

14.   This agreement shall be governed by the laws and procedures of England and the High Court in London shall be the Court of Jurisdiction.

For and on behalf of the Proprietor
VERNON COLEMAN

....
Duly Authorised

For and on behalf of the Publisher
OR AM PUBLISHING HOUSE LTD.

....
Duly Authorised

For and on behalf of the Agents
I. PIKARSKI LTD.

....
Duly Authorised

♦ Make sure you keep a log of all the foreign contracts you issue, what money is due and when. It's very easy to overlook payments due on signature and publication. If you work with foreign agents then they should be able to chase things up on your behalf.

FINANCIAL TIP

THE WORLD IS A BIG PLACE

The market for foreign rights is huge – and constantly growing. My books have sold in over 20 languages and over 50 different countries around the world. Advances and royalties from some countries may be small – but all those $1,500 and $1,000 advances add up.

early 1980s. I remember producing a series of *Home Doctor* cassettes back in the days when information was fed into computers by cassette. This was before diskettes. The *Home Doctor* tapes and a computer version of my book *Aspirin or Ambulance* were sold in 26 countries and were, I believe, the world's first attempt at multimedia publishing.

There was, however, a rather large snag. We didn't make any money. I suspect that the explanation for this may simply have been that there weren't enough people with computers to make the software an attractive commercial proposition.

In the middle and late 1980s I started writing, recording and selling audio cassettes. There was quite a good market for these but I never really fell in love with audio cassettes for the simple reason that even if I spoke quite quickly I couldn't get much more than three or four thousand words on each side of a cassette. Since VAT had to be added to the audio cassettes the final sale price was much the same as the price of a book and I never felt that audio tapes offered good value.

My main objection to audio cassettes was, however, very simple: they weren't books. I am a book author and I like writing books. I therefore abandoned the recording and selling of audio cassettes.

When the Internet appeared we arranged for a 36 page catalogue of our books to appear in an ethereal shopping arcade. But we sold hardly any books and I abandoned the whole venture quite early on.

Today, I still don't know of anyone (other than people in the computer business and confidence tricksters) who makes money out of the Internet. The Internet is a huge messy playground but as a selling medium it seems to me to be pretty useless. I am perfectly prepared to believe that it may become more useful in a few years time but for the time being I am happy to continue with my apparently old fashioned approach to publishing.

If you wish to play around with the Internet for fun then please do so. But I do not think that it currently offers a realistic route for the marketing and sale of books.

4. SELLING NAMES AND ADDRESSES

Once you have acquired a database containing a large number of names and addresses of customers you can consider selling those names and addresses to other businesses who are in, or wish to enter, direct mail selling. You can either do this yourself or via a list broker.

Some mail order companies make most of their money through selling names and addresses. We don't. We consider ourselves to be first and foremost a publishing house. If you do decide to sell your names then you should ensure that any customers who do not wish to receive direct mail are removed from your mailing list. We add a note to all our despatch letters inviting customers to let us know if they do not wish to receive mail from other companies.

5. START A NEWSLETTER

Once your book publishing business has become successful you may feel a desire to maintain regular contact with your readers. The easiest way to do this is through a newsletter.

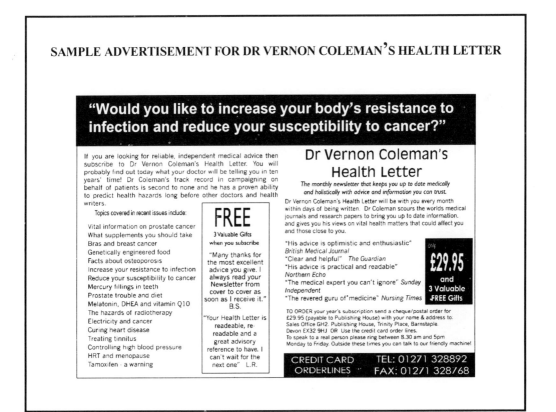

INTRODUCTORY LETTER FOR SUBSCRIBERS TO DR VERNON COLEMAN'S HEALTH LETTER

Dear Subscriber,

There is much, much more to life than simple good health. But good health is the foundation upon which everything else rests. Without good health none of us can enjoy life to the full.

We know more about staying healthy - and fighting disease - than at any other time in history. But finding the truth about medical matters is just as difficult as it has ever been. In some ways the explosion in research and the increased availability of medical information have made the truth even more difficult to find.

Who do you trust? How can you tell whether or not a doctor is being paid to do or say something by a drug company with a product to sell? How can you be sure that the doctor advocating a particular treatment technique is not just trying to win another patient? And how do you compare different medical and surgical techniques?

Doctors who practise as surgeons invariably claim that surgery has all the answers whereas doctors who practise as physicians will often argue that surgery is barbaric, clumsy and dangerous and should only be used as a last resort. Who is right?

The problem with finding the truth about health matters is that doctors tend to sing the tune they have been trained to sing. If you are suffering from cancer then a surgeon will sing the praises of surgery and a radiotherapist will sing the praises of radiotherapy. But which is the right treatment for you?

It is easy to draw an analogy between finding impartial, well informed medical advice and finding impartial, well informed financial advice.

If you have a sum of money to invest and you ask a bond specialist to recommend a safe investment he will suggest a bond. If you talk to a stockbroker he will advise that you invest directly in shares. If you talk to an insurance company man he will want to sell you an insurance policy. And if you talk to a bank manager - hoping that he will able to guide you to the correct type of investment - the chances are that he will not know enough about what is available and feasible to be able to offer you the accurate, impartial advice that you need.

A family doctor is the medical equivalent of a bank manager. In an ideal world you would be able to ask a general practitioner to take over, guide you and offer you accurate and impartial advice about health matters.

But most family doctors are probably too busy to have the time to spare. And, to be honest, they are probably not up to date.

In the old days most patients preferred to see an older more experienced doctor because they believed that he knew more and would have balanced his medical training with a good deal of acquired wisdom and common sense. But if a doctor qualified more than five years ago then the chances are that just about everything he learned at medical school is out of date - and that everything he has learned since he left medical school has been taught to him by drug companies. Just keeping up to date is a pretty full time job these days - and most family doctors just don't have the time.

Of course, there is one big difference between seeking investment advice and seeking medical advice. If you receive poor investment advice then the worst that is likely to happen is that you will lose your money. But if you receive bad medical advice then you may lose your life.

And that brings me to the purpose of my Health Letter.

I have argued for the whole of my professional life that every individual should have the right to take control of his or her own health.

You should make the decisions about what happens to you. It is your life and only you can know what is right for you. You should not allow anyone to make vital decisions for you. Doctors make mistakes and most doctors have a vested interest of some kind.

Obviously, if you follow this philosophy then you will need information and advice. And that is where I believe I can help you.

Every month I will bring you up to date information and advice gathered from specialists and clinics around the world. My aim is simply to keep you informed so that you will be better able to make decisions about your own health and health care. The final responsibility should still be yours.

The advice I will give you will always be the advice I would take myself - or the advice I would give to a someone close to me.

Although I used to be a general practitioner I no longer practise medicine and so have no allegiance to any particular branch of the profession. I can approach each subject relatively free of prejudices or preconceived notions. I never provide endorsements or do advertisements for particular products. My only source of income is providing advice for readers.

And although I have grave reservations about many aspects of modern medicine I refuse to throw out the good with the bad. I believe that orthodox medicine sometimes offers the best form of treatment and that alternative medicine sometimes offers the best. I believe in a 'pick and mix' philosophy. I am happy to take the best from any form of medicine.

I cannot, of course, give specific advice in my Health Letter. It would be irresponsible and foolhardy for me to try. I'm not trying to take over your doctor's job - that would be lunatic. After all, one of my aims is to help you get the best out of your doctor.

And it would also be quite against my philosophy to try and give you specific advice; my aim is to help you take responsibility for your own health.

I will give you the best information and the best general advice I can. And because I believe that good health involves more than just a healthy body - it also requires a healthy mind and spirit too - my Health Letter will deal with the mind and the spirit as well as the body.

You and I may never meet. But I hope that through my Health Letter we can become good friends with a common aim: continued good health for those we love and care about.

Vernon Coleman

SAMPLE PAGE FROM DR VERNON COLEMAN'S HEALTH LETTER

European Medical Journal

Dr. Vernon Coleman's Health Letter

Vol. 3 No.4
Nov 1998

Vernon Coleman MB ChB DSc practised medicine for ten years. He has written over 80 books which have been translated into 22 languages.

CONTENTS

Must where you live determine when you die? ...p1

Testing environmental chemicals ...p3

Fraudulent medical research ...p5

Insecticide sprays - an air travel hazard ...p6

Serotonin ...p7

Animal fat ...p7

Essiac ...p8

Pernicious anaemia ...p8

Atrial fibrillation ...p9

Omega-3 fatty acids ...p9

Asthma and vaccines ...p9

Underactive thyroid ...p9

How to cut down on your sleep requirement ...p10

Transplanted cancer ...p10

Beware of salt...p10

Updates ...p11

Must Where You Live Determine When You Die?

A recent British study has shown that people who live in rural areas live longer than people who live in cities. Moreover, (and even more important) the inequalities are getting rapidly wider.

These differences are not minor - they are enormously significant.

For example, residents of Glasgow (a city in Scotland) are already 66% more likely to die prematurely than people living in rural Dorset (a county in Southern England).

The British Government has acknowledged the differences and is planning to look for explanations. But since the explanations are already pretty obvious it is clear that the politicians are, as usual, eager to avoid confronting real issues which may cost money and cause political embarrassment.

Some may claim that these differences in life expectation are largely a result of variations in wealth. The poor are, after all, more likely to live in overcrowded conditions in big cities and more likely to eat an inadequate, fat rich diet.

But wealth is not the primary factor.

Even poor people who live in the country frequently live longer than town and city dwellers.

The truth is that many of the life style choices which lead to a longer life are available to everyone - and not dependent on wealth.

Why Living In A City Is Bad For Your Health

Here are my views on the real reasons why living in a city is bad for your health (together with ways in which city dwellers can improve their life expectancy):

1. Despite attempts to reduce pollution, the air that is breathed in heavily populated areas is still polluted - largely by cars. There is no easy solution to this problem - masks

Most people in newspaper, magazine and book publishing turn up their noses at newsletter publishing. They think it is a fringe activity. They regard it as something people do for a hobby. It isn't. I know of one newsletter in the USA which sells over 500,000 copies a year. Each subscriber pays around $60. I know of another newsletter with 5,000 subscribers – each paying around £250 a year.

If you have an expertise which you are prepared to share with others – and you want to keep total publishing control yourself – then you can write, publish and sell a regular newsletter. Publishing House produces and distributes *Dr Vernon Coleman's Health Letter* every month. Our newsletter already has readers in 17 different countries. Your newsletter does not need to be extravagantly produced. Indeed, many newsletter writers believe that it is an advantage for a newsletter to look homely, friendly and approachable. A book should look like a book but a newsletter can look as if it has been put together in the spare bedroom (even if it hasn't been).

6. EXPORT SALES

At some point you may find yourself being contacted by a foreign distributor wanting to know if he can sell copies of your books in his country. This has happened to us quite frequently but only on one occasion has it proved profitable (and then the profit really only came through the fact that the increased sales enabled us to increase our print runs and therefore lower our production prices).

There are several snags with export sales.

The first is that you will almost inevitably be dealing with someone you have never met.

Second, is the fact that it is extremely expensive to send books long distances. Books are exceptionally heavy items but they are also easily damaged and so they have to be crated up and protected with vast quantities of bubble wrap or something similar.

The third problem is the fact that you will have to fill in so much damned paperwork to move books out of your country and into his country that you will begin to wonder whether the whole exercise is worthwhile.

Fourth, comes the fact that you will probably be paid in a foreign currency. You will, therefore, have to make an allowance for the currency risk. Naturally, a whole series of banks will want to share in your good fortune in selling your books abroad. Banks may well be the only people to benefit from your efforts. Indeed, it is possible that your best chance of profiting from exporting your books will be to buy bank shares.

The fifth problem is the fact that all these problems will mean that your books will almost certainly have to be priced at a higher level than the local market can bear. In the US books are very cheap and imports usually seem horrendously expensive.

The sixth problem is the fact that you may have a considerable amount of difficulty in persuading your foreign distributor to send you any money. This problem can usually be avoided by insisting that they send you money before you send them books. Distributors who refuse to do this can safely be avoided on the grounds that they would have probably never come up with the money anyway.

The best solution for everyone is to try and sell reprint rights rather than trying to export copies of books. You can send artwork, plates, mechanicals and all the other stuff needed to print copies of your book after you have received an advance against future royalties.

7. PUBLISH OTHER PEOPLE'S BOOKS

This is, I readily confess, the one part of this book about which I know nothing.

Since I first started publishing my own books my office has regularly received manuscripts, typescripts, disks and letters from authors wanting me to publish their books. People send me novels, autobiographies and books of non fiction. Some of the authors who want me to publish their book are first timers. Others are seasoned professionals who have published a number of books with so called 'commercial' publishers.

All these manuscripts are returned to their authors with a letter wishing them the best of luck and explaining that we simply do not have the time to publish other people's books at the moment. And anyway, I still very much consider myself an author not a publisher.

But the important point as far as this book is concerned is that if I wanted to publish other peoples books I would have absolutely no difficulty in finding plenty of suitable material. Some of the manuscripts we are sent need a great deal of work. But others are excellent and could be published at a profit. It is my sincere hope that this book will encourage many people who might otherwise put their unpublished manuscript into a drawer to try self publishing.

Publishing will become stronger when more authors are publishing their own books. Maybe the conglomerates will sit up and take notice of what is happening (and become a little more daring) when they realise that controversial, spiky, passionate books do sell.

8. NEVER STOP WATCHING AND LEARNING

Always be prepared to learn from others. Every time you meet or read about someone successful – whose work or life you admire – observe them and learn from what they do. Ask yourself what it is that they are trying to do (if you get the chance you could ask them). Find out their philosophies. Find out what drives them. And write down everything you learn. (Writing things down is the best way to remember them).

Remember that every aspect of business life that can be measured can also be improved. And every aspect of business life (efficiency, sales per particular effort, profitability etc.) can be measured. You can only measure if you ask questions. And remember that you must ask the right questions. The quality of the questions you ask will have a fundamental effect on the quality of the answers you receive.

The single most important question in business (as in life) is: "Why?" The second most important question is: "So what?"

Only by constantly questioning yourself and those who are working with you will you minimise your errors and improve your business.

At regular intervals you should assess your current marketing programmes. Ask yourself how much effort you are putting into each programme – and how much of your business comes from that programme. You may discover some surprising truths about your business. For example, you may find that you are putting a lot of effort into a marketing area which isn't really worthwhile.

You should ask yourself why people bought from you in the past and why they buy from you now. Ask yourself whether you are still offering as good a service as you used to offer. If you have lost some of your original hope, passion and ingenuity then maybe there is something you can do to regain those lost values.

At least once a year you should sit down and remember why you first started publishing your own books. You should ask yourself what you wanted to do. Try to decide if your aims have changed. And ask yourself how well you are satisfying those early targets.

You should ask yourself what you can offer readers that no one else can offer. What is your greatest advantage over your competitors? What is it about your business that makes you proudest? Are you proud of the books you are writing? Are you proud of how your books look? Are you proud of the service you are providing? (You should, of course, be able to answer "yes" to all those questions.)

YOUR SPECIAL ADVANTAGE

MARKETING IDEA

You must decide what is special about the book you are selling – and the way you are selling it. Obviously, if you are selling through the mail then one big advantage you have to offer is that your customers don't have to catch a bus or drive into their nearest town and try to park. They don't have to go into a bookshop, look through all the dross laid out on the display tables, queue and then wait to order a decent book from you. Their book purchase comes post free and is guaranteed. If they want to send it back they get a full refund. What have they got to lose? Once you have isolated the special advantage to the customer of doing business with you then you must tell – and remind – the customer of this advantage.

9. ALWAYS TRY TO MAKE YOUR BUSINESS GROW

You should always be thinking of expanding your business. The business which does not expand and grow and change and adapt will atrophy and die. There are four fundamental ways to expand a business.

First, you can find more customers. To do this you will have to make your product or service better known to a wider range of potential customers. You may be able to do this by advertising or by publicity or by encouraging your present customers to help you find new customers.

Second, you can encourage each customer to spend more money with you every time they buy (usually by buying more books).

Third, you can encourage your existing customers to come back to you more often.

And fourth, you can ask your customers to spread news about your book to their friends. Once your customers start telling their friends and relatives about your book then your business will boom.

Remember that the best way to grow is through word of mouth. Very large businesses know that however much money they spend promoting a new product (such as a new movie or compact disk) the ultimate success or failure of the item will depend not upon the extent of the promotional expenditure but upon whether or not people like the product and recommend it to their friends.

Having said that I cannot end this section without a small warning. Decide how big you want to be – and don't let your business get so big that it stops being fun. After just a few years of self publishing we found that we were employing seven or eight people and running a proper business.

The turnover was terrific and the profits were excellent but there were problems. Finding the right staff, and keeping them all happy, began to take up more and more of our time. Sue Ward (who was running Publishing House before it was Publishing House) was spending more and more of her time working as a personnel officer. (I think the politically correct term is human resources officer – a term which I regard as far more offensive than 'personnel officer'; talking of people as 'human resources' makes it sound as though they are stored in a large warehouse and taken out as and when they are needed). The bigger the business became the more administration we found we had to do. Wages, holidays and working rotas all had to be coordinated. We were constantly buying advertisements, checking copy, ordering reprints and dealing with all the associated problems. A crisis at the printers, with a subsequent delay in the delivery date of another batch of books, would mean that we had to send out letters of apology to thousands of people. At one point the office became so frantic that £4,500 worth of cheques were lost (either stolen by an intruder or thrown away into the rubbish).

And, of course, the paperwork and the accounts required to keep the government happy also grew. (And, at the end of each financial year 40% of the hard earned profits were taken by the government to spend on things that neither of us approved of.)

Eventually Sue and I decided that although we very much enjoyed publishing books, and obviously wanted to carry on making a decent profit, we really didn't want to spend our lives running a large business and keeping a lot of employees happy.

So we downsized.

Today we run a much smaller business. But we're happier.

10. PUBLIC LENDING RIGHT

As an author you are entitled to a small income calculated according to the number of times your book is borrowed from public libraries. This money comes directly from the government and so you should take every penny you are entitled to. (You will, of course, pay tax on it in due course so the government will get some of its own money back.)

The annual cheque from the Public Lending Right Office is extremely welcome but it is also good to receive a print out from the PLR office showing how many people have borrowed your books from public libraries (see page 79).

To avoid spending too much of the available money on administration a small group of public libraries is used to check on library usage and your cheque is then calculated by adjusting this figure for the national number of libraries.

11. PROMOTIONAL GIFTS

Many publishers make a good deal of their income by selling their books to companies who want 'give aways' for their customers. For example, if you publish a book about Paris or about France you might be able to persuade a travel company, a villa rental company, a credit card company or some other organisation to buy copies from you to give away. If you do this the chances are that you will have to discount the book heavily. The advantage to you is that if you can arrange the sale before you finalise your print order you will be able to print more copies and therefore bring down your unit print costs.

GLOSSARY OF PUBLISHING AND PRINTING TERMS

ADVANCE INFORMATION SHEET

Promotional sheet describing a forthcoming book. Contains brief details of the book (author, publisher, price and a short resume of the contents). AI sheets are posted to bookshops and others likely to buy the book.

BACK END SALES

A sale made to a customer who has already bought a book from you. Most of the real profits to be made out of mail order publishing are made through 'back end sales'.

BACKLIST

Previously published books which are still in print and therefore still available. Many orthodox, traditional publishers pay remarkably little attention to their backlist titles and ignore the opportunity for long term, steady sales – and a long term, steady income.

BAR CODE

A code representing the ISBN and the selling price of the book which is printed on the back cover of the book and makes a mess of the design. Bar codes can be read by machines but not by humans unless they are very, very clever and have such empty lives that they have nothing better to do than learn how to read them.

BLEED

A printing term. When whatever is printed on a page runs right up to the very edge of the paper it is said to bleed.

BINDER'S OVERS

The extra covers you need to supply to the company who will finish your book. These are needed in case any covers or jackets are damaged during the final process.

BLOCK

Blocking is the process used to imprint the book title, author's name and publisher's name onto the hardcover of a book (most usually found on the spine).

BLURB

Information found on book covers and jackets which describes the contents of the book – and usually includes something about the author too.

Body copy
The main text within an advertisement.

Book
According to UNESCO a book is a non periodical publication which contains 49 or more pages, excluding the cover.

Book fair
Places (often abroad and most notably in Frankfurt, Germany) where self important people who know very little about anything and much less about books rush around looking extremely important and selling each other rights in books none of them have read.

Brass
A metal stamp used to impress the book title, author's name and publisher's name onto the hard cover or a book (usually down the spine).

Bromide
A photographic image of artwork to be used in a book, catalogue or advertisement.

Buyer
Person in a bookshop who has the responsibility for selecting and ordering books for stock. (Alternatively, a sensible, thoughtful, well read, sophisticated individual who hands over money in exchange for one of my or your books.)

Camera ready copy
Material which is ready to be photographed to make a litho plate ready for printing.

Carriage
Shipping books from somewhere to somewhere. As the publisher you will almost certainly be responsible for carriage costs.

Carriage – forward
The bookseller chooses how to have the book delivered to him. And he pays the carriage costs. You will not be surprised that this is a rare method of moving books from publisher to bookseller.

Carriage – free
The publisher pays for the delivery to the bookshop. And as a reward for paying, the publisher can choose the route (e.g. through the Post Office or a carrier).

CASE BOUND
A hard back book.

CAST OFF
- Counting the number of words or characters in a typescript in order to work out how many pages the book will be. Computers do the counting for you these days. (Bless their silicone hearts).
- Calculating how many pages a chunk of copy will occupy when printed in a chosen typeface.
- Also a knitting term which I do not pretend to understand.

CHAIN BOOKSHOP
A bookshop that belongs to a chain of stores.

CHARACTER
A space, letter, symbol or punctuation mark.

CHARTER BOOKSHOP
Alleged to be a rather superior sort of bookshop with a good variety of stock.

CLOSED MARKET
If you sell Russian rights in a book to a Russian publisher and no one else can publish that book in Russia then Russia becomes a closed market as far as that book is concerned.

COLOPHON
A publisher's logo. Makes the publisher feel important but is a waste of time and money and is unlikely to sell you any more books. (How many books do you buy because you like the colophon?)

COMMISSION
A percentage of the money brought in by an agent and paid to him as a reward for his services.

COPY
Words.

COPYRIGHT
The exclusive right to material (usually written). Copyright belongs to an author unless he has specifically sold it someone else. No author should ever, ever sell his copyright. He should lease it or sell the right to use his work.

copies of your book. Ideally a counter pack should sit next to the till so that customers see it at their most vulnerable (when they have their wallets or purses open). Bookshops receive so many counter packs that yours is likely to be thrown straight into the bin.

CREDIT NOTE

Someone owes someone money but doesn't want to part with hard cash. If you owe a bookseller money (because he has returned books to you and doesn't want to buy anything else you have for sale) then you can give him a credit note instead of sending him a cheque. He will be thrilled by this.

DATABASE

Information kept in a computer file. Your most important database will be the list of names and addresses of your customers. If you keep this on a computer then you should keep several copies (regularly updated) in safe places.

DESK TOP PUBLISHING

A computer, some software and a printer. You can publish commercially using DTP as long as you hire a real printer to produce your books. If you use your own back bed-room printer then whatever you produce will always look rather amateurish. Sorry.

DIRECT COSTS

The costs that can be related specifically to one book. Direct costs include printing and binding costs, for example.

DISCOUNT

The amount the publisher knocks off the retail price when selling to a bookshop or wholesaler or good customer or anyone prepared to hand over hard cash.

DISTRIBUTOR

Organisation which stocks books and supplies them to bookshops. You can hire a professional distributor to warehouse your books and send them out to bookshops and members of the public. They will charge you a fee for every book they send out and you will have to send them all the instructions. There is, inevitably, a good chance that things will go wrong. If you want to save money and have the space to store your own books you can handle your distribution yourself.

DUES

Orders bookshops place with a publisher for books which are not yet available – either because they have not yet been printed or because they are being reprinted.

Dump bin

A large free standing cardboard container which occupies a good deal of floor space in a bookshop and sells the books of a single author of publisher. You can have dump bins made if you like but they will probably end up being dumped in the bin.

Edition

An edition of a book includes all the copies which are printed without any significant changes to the text. One edition may, therefore, include several impressions or printings.

Electronic stock control (EPOS)

A cashier wipes a special pen over the barcode and a computer somewhere takes note. Electronic stock control enables bookshop buyers to see which books are selling and which are not – it makes it easier for bookshops to return books to the publisher.

Em

The amount of space occupied by the letter 'm' in your chosen typeface and point size. The letter 'm' is chosen because it is the widest letter in the alphabet.

Embargo

If you have a red hot press release and you want to stop editors using it before a certain time then you can put an 'embargo' on it. Theoretically, this will protect your information and make sure that one newspaper doesn't use the story as an exclusive – thereby stopping other newspapers from running the story. Sadly, editors tend not to take much notice of press embargoes these days. Publishers used to put embargoes on books sent out for review but this is rather a waste of time these days since literary editors, being an unusually low lot, no longer take any notice of such things.

En dash

You should know the difference between an en dash and a hyphen.

This is an en dash: –
This is a hyphen: -

Hyphens are used, not surprisingly, in hyphenated words such as mass-media, old-fashioned and en-suite. En dashes should be used – you may have deduced – to separate text (e.g. to set off parenthetical material or breaks in thought). There are heaps of copyediting rules about en and em dashes. We ignore most of them.

Estimate

A guess at the cost of a project. Printers' estimates are probably slightly more reliable than builders' estimates. Always get a firm quote before you commit to a project.

FIRM SALE

This is what every publisher wants to hear. It means that a bookseller who is ordering books isn't going to want to send them back. He is buying them 'firm sale' and agreeing to keep them even if he can't sell them. (When a small publisher sells books 'firm sale' it usually either means that the bookseller already has customers for the books or that the publisher is giving a massive discount.)

FOOTER

A section of text printed as a separate item at the very bottom of a page (this text may also be reproduced on several pages and is then known as a 'running footer').

FORMAT

The shape and size of a publication. The format also includes the number of pages and the type of binding.

FULFILMENT

Receiving, processing and dispatching orders from customers.

FULFILMENT HOUSE

Company which does the fulfilment of orders for you (at a price).

GROSS PROFIT

The total value of book sales minus major overheads such as printing. Overhead costs are not taken out of gross profit. When overhead costs are removed you are (hopefully) left with net profit.

GUTTER

The part of a page nearest the spine of a book, newspaper or magazine.

HEADER

A section of text printed as a separate item at the very top of a page (this text may also be reproduced on several pages and is then known as a 'running header').

IMPOSITION

An arrangement of all the pages of a book, in the correct order and ready for printing. When you get to this stage it is just about too late to do anything so you can stop worrying.

IMPRESSION

All the copies of a book which are printed at one time without the printing plates being altered.

IMPOSITION

The way in which pages are laid out on a large printing plate so that when the printed sheet is folded the pages run in the correct order.

IMPRINT

The number under which a publishing house issues its books. At Publishing House we have three imprints: European Medical Journal (EMJ), Chilton Designs (CD) and Blue Books (BB). We use the EMJ for books on health and medicine, CD for fiction and Blue Books for everything else.

INDIRECT COSTS

Costs which cannot be related directly to a specific title. Telephone and heating costs are indirect. (Of course if you only have one title then all your costs could reasonably be described as 'direct'.)

IN HOUSE

Work you do yourself – as opposed to work which is put out to an outside organisation. So, if you are designing a book cover yourself you could describe this task as being kept 'in house'.

INSERT

A promotional leaflet inserted into a periodical. It usually stays there until the periodical is placed on the newsagents shelf when it falls onto the floor.

INVOICE VALUE

The amount shown on an invoice. This will usually be the retail value of the books, minus the discount agreed with or generously given to the bookseller or wholesaler.

ISBN

Stands for International Standard Book Number. Every book has a ten digit number these days. The ISBN helps to identify a book if it gets lost a long way from home. The first group of numbers may tell you the country of origin. The second group of numbers allegedly defines the publisher. The third group apparently describes the book (including the edition and whether it is hardback or paperback). And the fourth group is said to be a check on all the others.

ISSN
An eight figure identification number given to a periodical. The letters ISSN stand for International Standard Serial Number.

LAMINATION
A clear, protective film applied to a book cover or jacket

LANDSCAPE
The shape of a publication or photograph when the width exceeds the height.

LIBRARY SUPPLIER
Rather surprisingly, a firm which specialises in supplying books to libraries.

LIMP
This term is usually used to describe a paperback which has pretensions and, because it is made with a slightly better cover, is a sort of half way house between a paperback and a hard back.

LIST
The titles a publisher has for sale. Our list include all the books published under our three imprints. If you are publishing just one book to start with then your list will be very short but it will still be a list.

LIST BROKER
A company or individual who sells mailing lists of names and addresses to companies or individuals who want to send out a direct mail promotion.

MAILSHOT
When promotional leaflets are sent out to potential book buyers.

MAILSORT
Royal Mail scheme which allows you to do a huge amount of work in return for a small reduction in postage costs.

MARKETING
All those activities which are designed to ensure that a book is bought by as many people as possible. Your sales, distribution, advertising and promotional departments (probably all you) will be gathered together under 'marketing'.

MARK UP (1)
Preparing a manuscript for the typesetter by scribbling little messages all over it.

Mark up (2)

Pushing up the price of a book because you realise that you have screwed up and forgotten to include some costs when working out your publication price. Marking up your price may then enable you to discount the price.

Media buyer

A professional who earns a living buying advertising space for clients. The media buyer makes his money from commissions paid by the magazines and newspapers in which his clients buy space.

Minimum order

Large, snotty publishers will sometimes only deal with a bookshop if they send a 'minimum order' (e.g. for 10 or 20 books). Publishing House has a minimum order of one. We are not too proud or important to sell books one at a time.

Net profit

Anything left over after all the costs of production and the overheads have been deducted. Large publishing companies don't usually have to worry about this because they don't make any profit. Hopefully, you will.

Net receipts

The amount of money a publisher receives after the cost of postage or carriage has been deducted.

Not yet published

If you get bookshop orders for a book that you haven't yet published you write NYP on the order and send it back. The bookseller will either know what you mean or think you are just rude and your initials are NYP.

On costs

General costs (heat, light, rates etc.) that are shared between all the books being published by one publisher.

On consignment

Some publishers are so utterly desperate to sell their books that they will let the bookshops have them for free (on consignment) trusting that if any books are sold they will eventually be paid for them.

Open market

Part of the world where there is a free for all and anyone can sell a book – in whatever edition they like.

ORIGINATION

The various stages involved in preparing a manuscript for the printer. This may include editing, setting and providing the illustrations.

ORPHAN

The first line of a paragraph which is the last line on a page. Considered rather ungainly. You can usually get rid of an orphan by stretching the copy above and creating one more line.

OUT OF PRINT (O/P OR OOP)

Very sad news for the pessimistic author. But, good news for an optimistic author who sees an opportunity to sell the rights to another publisher or to bring out a new edition by himself.

OUT OF STOCK (O/S OR OOS)

The book isn't currently available but will be reprinted and therefore available before the end of the next millennium.

OVERHEADS

Salaries, office expenses and other general costs that do not relate to a specific book.

OZALIDS (A.K.A. BLUES)

The just before we start printing stuff. This is your very last chance to correct the mistake that will result in everyone suing you, laughing at you or buying copies of your book for the curiosity value.

PAGE

One side of a piece of paper in a book is a page. Both sides of the same piece of paper are a leaf. Two pages side by side are a double paged spread.

PAMPHLET

According to UNESCO a pamphlet contains less than 49 but more than 8 pages. (Below 8 pages it is presumably a leaflet).

PERFECT BINDING

Doesn't refer to the quality of the binding but to the fact that the back bits of the various signatures of the book are trimmed and then glued to the inside of the cover. Perfect binding is more expensive than simply stapling the pages together but cheaper than sewing. If you bend back a perfectly bound book you may crack it and if you do the pages will then all fall out.

POINT OF SALE

Promotional material designed to be displayed in bookshops in order to try to sell books. Usually kept in a back room where it won't get in the way of customers.

PORTRAIT

The shape of a publication or photograph when the height exceeds the width.

POSTLIMS

Printed pages that come at the end of the book, using up pages that would otherwise be blank and therefore a waste of paper. Many large, snooty publishers leave these pages blank. We always put advertisements for our books on the postlim pages.

PRELIMS

The pages of a book that precede the real stuff. Like the short travelogues and news items that used to be shown in the cinema. Prelims are usually paginated in roman numerals to show that the book hasn't really started yet and that the publisher knows about roman numerals.

PRESS RELEASE

A document sent out by publishers and thrown away by journalists.

PRINT RUN

The number of copies of a book published in one go.

PRODUCTION LEDGER

Big publishers keep a record of all the expenditure incurred by a particular title – and then check this against their estimates. This is, however, exceedingly boring and so we don't bother (but don't tell our printers).

PRO FORMA INVOICE

An invoice that must be paid before the publisher will part with the book or books. If you aren't sure that the bookseller will pay you then send him a pro-forma invoice.

PROMOTION

Advertising and publicity designed to sell more books.

PROOFS

A sign that something is happening and that the printer hasn't forgotten about your book. If you are producing your own camera ready copy using a desk top publishing package then you will also produce your own proofs. You will save a great deal of money if you do all your planned corrections before your book goes to the printer. Just remember that when the printer starts work every new comma or corrected error will cost you money.

PUBLICATION DATE

Moveable feast. The official date on which the book will go on sale to the public. Newspapers and other periodicals are not officially allowed to review a book before publication date. No one takes any notice of publication dates. Bookshops sell books when they get them and periodicals review them when they have the space. A publication date does, however, give a publisher and an author (in my and your case the same person) a chance to have a good meal and celebrate. You can alter the publication date if you need to fit in with a magazine schedule and they say that they will not run an extract or a review if they are going to be too far after your publication date. Don't tell anyone but some of our books have several publication dates.

PUBLISHED PRICE

List price – or the price at which a book is due to be sold.

RATE CARD

The price at which publishers like to sell advertising space in their publications. No self respecting publisher should pay rate card unless he is deliberately trying to go bankrupt as quickly as possible.

READING

A rather sad occasion when an author reads bits of his book out loud to a small group of very loyal readers, the vast majority of whom could just as easily read the book for themselves.

RECTO

Right hand page. (The front of a leaf).

REMAINDERS

Books sold off cheap because they can't be sold off at their proper price. Remainder merchants will often pay pitiful, knock down prices for the books they buy (often only a tiny fraction of the print costs). However, some remainder merchants do pay more reasonable prices for the books they buy and it is not unknown for large publishers to deliberately publish books to sell in remainder shops and on the remainder tables of bookshops. I was shocked to the core when I heard that this happened.

REPRINT

A cause for celebration. Printing a second, third, fourth or even later impression of a book. If you want to tell a bookshop that a book is reprinting you can use the abbreviation R/P.

REPRINT LINE

Details of the reprint year which are added to the title page verso.

REVIEW COPY

Book sent out to newspapers or magazines. They will probably sell it to a friendly bookshop. They will probably not review it.

REVIEW SLIP

A small piece of paper containing details of the book being sent for review and asking the literary editor to send a copy of any review published. Pitiful really, isn't it?

RIGHTS

Every book has all sorts of rights. Paperback rights. Korean hardback rights. Portuguese book club rights. Film rights. Television rights. Radio rights. And so on. Successful, profitable publishing depends upon selling lots of rights.

ROYALTY

The percentage of the list price paid over to the author by a publisher.

SALE OR RETURN

The bookseller takes books, keeps them until they get battered and grubby and then sends them back to the publisher who throws them away. The sale or return policy is one of the main reason why big publishers don't make any money. When booksellers return books to big publishers they will usually accept payment as an extension of their credit. (In other words they send back one book they can't sell and, in exchange, receive a similarly valued supply of another book they probably won't be able to sell.) When booksellers return a book to a small publisher they will usually demand a refund in cash – arguing that there isn't anything else on the list that they want to stock. Demands for cash refunds should be strongly resisted.

SANS SERIF TYPE

A typeface which has no sort of twiddly stroke thing at the end of the line of a character.
This is a sample of sans serif face called Arial.

SEE SAFE

Books sent to a bookshop on the agreement that they may be returned for credit or for a supply of another book if they do not sell.

SELF ENDS

Binding term used to describe what happens when the first and last pages of a hardback book are stuck to the inside of cover board. This means you do not have to use another, separate four pages for endpapers and so this option can save you money if you have a few spare pages in your book. If you want fancy, coloured endpapers then you almost certainly won't be able to use this cheaper option.

SERIF
Type with a sort of twiddle thing at the end of every line of each character.
This book is set in a serif face called Times New Roman.

SHORT TERM
Advertising space which is left over and sold off cheaply close to the moment when the presses start to roll.

SIGNATURE
A folded sheet of printing, usually containing 16 or 32 pages. Books are made up of signatures and are, therefore, usually comprised of chunks of 16 or 32 pages.
If you are producing a booklet rather than a book then the smallest signature you can have is four pages (any smaller and you have a double-sided leaflet!).

SIGNING SESSION
Very sad occasion when an author arrives at a bookshop and the staff and their relatives rush round and round in circles giving him books to sign because no one has turned up.

SINGLE COPY
Sale of one copy of a book. (Publishers like to make up jargon).

SLEEPER (1)
A book that doesn't sell very quickly to start with but eventually sells well. If your book is a disaster you can always say that it is an incipient sleeper.

SLEEPER (2)
A name put into a mailing list so that the person selling the mailing list can tell if the list has been used more than once. (Or more times than have been paid for).

SOLUS POSITION
When there is just one advertisement on a whole page in a newspaper or magazine.

SPECIFICATIONS
The details of a book sent to a printer to get a quote.

SPINNER
Revolting display unit used in bookshops to display books.

STRIP IN
A term used to describe the process of replacing old material with new material on camera ready artwork.

SUBSCRIPTION ORDERS
Pre-publication orders for a book.

TELEORDERING
Clever electronic system enabling booksellers to send book orders to publishers via a central clearing house system.

TERMS
The discount and the credit period offered by a publisher to a bookseller.

TRADE SALES
Books sold through bookshops as opposed to books sold through greengrocers.

TURNOVER
The total value of books sold within a specific period (usually a year).

UNIT COST
The cost of producing all the copies of a single title divided by the number of copies printed. So if you have 1,000 books printed at a cost of £9,000 the unit cost is £9 and you are probably in big trouble.

UV VARNISH
Stands for ultra violet varnish which is applied like an ink during the printing process. Used on covers as an alternative to lamination. Check with your printer which finish he prefers as some knife trimmers (used to do the final trim on books) cause uv varnish to chip. Lamination is usually a bit more expensive than uv varnish.

VERSO
A left hand page.

WHOLESALER
Someone or a company who buys books in bulk from a publisher and then sells them on to bookshops and other retailers.

Wɪᴅᴏᴡ

A single line or, worse still, a single word at the top of a page. Doesn't look nice but can usually be eradicated by fiddling with the text on the previous page. Getting rid of a widow on one page usually creates an orphan (q.v.) or a widow on another page.

Let Dr Vernon Coleman Explain How To Conquer 9 Out Of 10 Illnesses Without Money Or Doctors.

It may sound too good to be true. But it is true. There is a free, doctor-approved secret with which you can, for the rest of your life, easily conquer 9 out of 10 illnesses without spending money or seeing a doctor.

When you have "Bodypower" most illnesses can be dealt with without pills or medicines and without orthodox or alternative therapies.

You can get better without spending time and money on doctors, specialists, acupuncturists, hypnotherapists or pills from the chemist – and without exposing yourself to hazardous and uncomfortable side effects.

We recently published a new edition of **Bodypower** – the sensational book by Dr Vernon Coleman which hit the Sunday Times bestseller list and the Bookseller chart too. This fascinating book, reprinted 9 times in the UK and sold in just about every country in the world, shows how 9 out of 10 illnesses can be treated without seeing a doctor.

As a bonus, **Bodypower** includes simple but effective tips on: How to stay slim for life – How to improve your figure – How to break bad habits – How to relax your body and mind – and much, much more.

If you think our claims for **Bodypower** are difficult to believe, read what the critics had to say about it:

'One of the most sensible treatises on personal survival that has ever been published. It sets out, in the simplest language, an enormous amount of knowledge in the easiest possible way.' Yorkshire Evening Post

'Don't miss it! Dr Coleman' theories could change your life...the revolutionary way to look better and feel younger.' Sunday Mirror

'...a self help manual for maintaining or regaining health using your own resources. Prolific and broadminded former general practitioner Vernon Coleman presents his evidence with clarity and evangelical fervour...' The Good Book Guide

'There are plenty of good books on health care in the shops and for starters I'd recommend Bodypower.' Woman's Own

'Stimulating, outspoken and easy to understand.' Oxford Mail

'If Bodypower really caught on, it could help to save the National Health Service from slow strangulation.' The Scotsman

'Despite my own medical training and knowledge of nature's devices, Dr Coleman made me think again.' BBC World Service

'If you've got Bodypower you may never need to visit your doctor again ' Slimmer

'...marvellously succinct ... refreshingly sensible.' The Spectator

AN INTERNATIONAL BESTSELLER

Bodypower
Paperback £9.95

PUBLISHING HOUSE, TRINITY PLACE, BARNSTAPLE, DEVON EX32 9HJ   TEL: 01271 328892

SPIRITPOWER
The Book and the Philosophy

We are all composed of three parts: body, mind and spirit. In *Bodypower* Vernon Coleman described the body's astonishing self-healing powers and explained how you can take advantage of those powers to stay healthy and to defeat nine out of ten physical illnesses. In the sequel *Mindpower* Vernon Coleman explored the powers of the mind, described how you can harness positive emotions and conquer destructive emotions and explained how you can use your mind to heal your body and teach yourself mental self defence. In *Spiritpower*, he deals with the third, and most abstract of the "body, mind, spirit" trilogy. He takes a pragmatic approach to this topic and explores the essential elements of a healthy spirit by examining individual liberty and personal freedom in the twentieth century.

This is a timely book which is sure to be met with as much enthusiasm as the first two publications in this trilogy of titles. It examines the reasons for our loss of freedom and personal dignity and describes how we can all regain our physical, mental and spiritual freedom.

EXTRACTS FROM SPIRITPOWER

- 'If there is anything more frustrating than having responsibility without the necessary authority, it must be coming face to face with people who have authority but no personal responsibility. *p 50*

- 'You must know who you are. Many people spend their entire lives trying to be someone they are not.' *p 138*

- 'Not until you know why you do something will you be able to do it effectively.' *p 149*

- 'Remember that you are now enjoying tomorrow's good old days.' *p 149*

- 'Providing your family with a constant supply of clean underwear is not a purpose for living.' *p 170*

- 'Work is anything you don't want to do. The more you don't want to do it, the more it becomes work.' *p 224*

- 'It is almost impossible to find anyone who has ever had a creative and worthwhile idea who has not been marginalised, ridiculed and persecuted by the relevant establishment.' *p 238*

- 'True friendship is an asset which will never tarnish and never devalue. And no one will ever be able to take it away from you.' *p 241*

Spiritpower HARDBACK £24.95

PUBLISHING HOUSE, TRINITY PLACE, BARNSTAPLE, DEVON EX32 9HJ   TEL: 01271 328892

Alice's Diary

Over 30,000 delighted readers from around the world have already bought this wonderful book which tells of a year in the life of a mixed tabby cat called Alice. She records the year's events and disasters with great humour and insight and at long last gives us a glimpse of what it is really like to be a cat! Delightfully illustrated throughout, *Alice's Diary* is an absolute must for animal and cat lovers everywhere.

Our files are bursting with letters from confirmed fans who write and tell us how much they have enjoyed this book.

"I bought Alice's Diary which was read and re-read by young and old members of my family and greatly enjoyed." (E. M., Cheshire)

"I felt I must put paw to paper to say how very much my human and myself enjoyed your Diary." (The W. family in West Sussex)

"Alice's Diary is one of the nicest books I have ever read. She has wonderful insight." (Mrs. J., London)

"I am delighted with Alice's Diary – I must have Alice's Adventures." (V.H., Grimsby)

GREAT GIFT IDEA!

REMEMBER – WE CAN POST BOOKS ANYWHERE IN THE WORLD ON YOUR BEHALF

Alice's Diary
£9.95 Hardback

Alice's Adventures

After the publication of her hugely successful first book, Alice was inundated with fan mail urging her to put pen to paper once more. The result is this, her second volume of memoirs in which she shares with us yet another exciting and eventful year in her life.

Alice's Adventures is full of the wry, witty observations on life which so delighted the readers of her first book, and the wonderful illustrations capture the most poignant moments of her year.

"...as far as Alice's Diary and Alice's Adventures are concerned, nothing would persuade me to part with my copies of these two books for I have had hours of delight in reading them."
(Miss W., Cheshire)

GREAT GIFT IDEA!

Alice's Adventures
£9.95 Hardback

PUBLISHING HOUSE, TRINITY PLACE, BARNSTAPLE, DEVON EX32 9HJ   TEL: 01271 328892

Know Yourself

'Understand Your Own Behaviour, Motivation And Strengths'

Not until you know yourself, and understand your own weaknesses, strengths and hidden driving forces, can you get the most out of life, says Dr Vernon Coleman. His fascinating book *Know Yourself* contains 940 questions and scores of psychological quizzes designed to help you get to know yourself better. Find out how impulsive, sensual and ruthless you are and then – in Part Two of the book – find out if you could run your own business or how well you would cope if you were shipwrecked! *Know Yourself* is so much fun that you won't realise just how much you're learning about yourself.

Quizzes include:

- *What sort of job is right for you?*
- *How creative are you?*
- *How good is your memory?*
- *How strong is your sex drive?*
- *What sort of partner is right for you?*
- *Are you a positive or negative thinker?*
- *Could you run the country?*
- *Are you a good lover?*
- *How intuitive are you?*
- *Will you ever be rich?*

- *Are you a hypochondriac?*
- *How reliable are you?*
- *How sociable are you?*
- *How tolerant are you?*
- *How vain are you?*
- *How trusting are you?*
- *Are you liberated?*
- *How impulsive are you?*
- *Are you jealous?*
- *Are you a workaholic?*

**GREAT
GIFT
IDEA!**

Know Yourself
Paperback £9.95

Alice And Other Friends

Thousands of readers have already discovered the joys of **Alice's Diary** and **Alice's Adventures** – two books by a mixed tabby cat which have sold thousands of copies and entranced animal lovers all over the world. Vernon Coleman 'helped' Alice write and illustrate these two books. Now, at last, here is Vernon Coleman's own account of life with Alice and her half sister Thomasina.

Charming, touching and intensely personal this book is packed with stories, anecdotes and reminiscences about Alice and the many other creatures Vernon Coleman has met, known and lived with. There are, of course, many personal stories about Vernon Coleman's four pet sheep. The book is liberally and beautifully illustrated with numerous line drawings by the author.

Alice and Other Friends
Hardback £12.95

PUBLISHING HOUSE, TRINITY PLACE, BARNSTAPLE, DEVON EX32 9HJ   TEL: 01271 328892

'For Sheer Relaxing Pleasure'

Over half a million readers have already discovered the joys of Vernon Coleman's series of novels based in and around the fictional village of Bilbury. These novels are in the tradition of the very best of English writing – full of gentle humour, anecdotes and colourful characters – just the thing for relaxing and unwinding. Anyone who enjoys a good book and likes country life will love the Bilbury series.

THE BILBURY CHRONICLES £12.95 HARDBACK

A young doctor arrives to begin work in the small village of Bilbury which is home to some memorable characters who have many a tale to tell. Vernon Coleman weaves a superb story full of humour and anecdotes transporting you back to the days of old-fashioned village life where you never needed to lock your door, and when a helping hand was only ever a moment away.

"I am just putting pen to paper to say how very much I enjoyed The Bilbury Chronicles. I just can't wait to read the others"
(Mrs K, Cambs)

"I have just finished reading The Bilbury Chronicles and I would like to take this opportunity to congratulate Mr. Coleman on writing such a wonderful book which is both entertaining and touching. I now enclose an order for Bilbury Grange"
(A.L.,Ballymena)

"I am writing to tell you how much I enjoyed reading your book 'The Bilbury Chronicles'. Thanking you sincerely for giving me so much pleasure."
(Mrs A H, Ramsgate)

**GREAT
GIFT
IDEA!**

~

BILBURY GRANGE £12.95 HARDBACK

The second novel in the Bilbury series sees the now married doctor moving into his new home – a vast and rambling country house in desperate need of renovation. With repair bills soaring and money scarce, the doctor and his new wife look for additional ways to make ends meet. Another super novel in this series – perfect for hours of escapism!

"I found the book to be brilliant. I felt as though I was part of the community. Please keep me informed of any more in this excellent series"
(I.C.,Cleethorpes)

"A cornucopia of colourful characters help to weave a rich tapestry of village life subtly tempered with gentle humour ... the mixture of rural beauty, human nature and the odd whisper of nostalgia combine to make this book a real delight"
(Western Gazette)

PUBLISHING HOUSE, TRINITY PLACE, BARNSTAPLE, DEVON EX32 9HJ   TEL: 01271 328892

The Village Cricket Tour

The Village Cricket Tour
hardback £12.95

This superb novel tells the story of a team of amateur cricketers who spend two weeks of their summer holidays on tour in the West Country. It proves to be a most eventful fortnight full of mishaps and adventures as the team play their way around the picturesque coastline of Devon and Cornwall. A marvellous gift for a cricket lover. Over 15,000 copies sold.

'The only word to describe (this book) is hilarious. It is the funniest book about cricket that I have ever read. In fact it is the funniest book I have read since Three Men in a Boat and Vernon Coleman's style is very similar to that of Jerome K Jerome. Anyone interested in cricket will find this book irresistible.'
(Chronicle & Echo)

'I enjoyed it immensely. He has succeeded in writing a book that will entertain, a book that will amuse and warm the cockles of tired old hearts.'
(Peter Tinniswood, Punch)

'Coleman is a very funny writer'
(This England)

Thomas Winsden's Cricketing Almanack

Thomas Winsden's Cricketing Almanack
hardback £9.95

A new edition of this much-loved spoof version of Wisden – the cricketing "Bible". Includes such comical gems as: How to clap – Food and drink for cricketers – Etiquette for spectators – Prayers for cricketers – and much more

'Its pages are witty and very funny. A treat.'
(Cricket World)

The Man Who Inherited a Golf Course

The Man Who Inherited a Golf Course
hardback £12.95

Trevor Dukinfield, the hero of this novel, wakes up one morning to discover that he is the owner of his very own golf club – fairways, bunkers, clubhouse and all. This unexpected present lands in Trevor's lap as a result of a distant uncle's will which he discovers, to his dismay, contains several surprising clauses. To keep the club he must win an important match – and he's never played a round of golf in his life!

'This scenario is tailor made for Vernon Coleman's light and amusing anecdotes about country life and pursuits. His fans will lap it up'
(Sunday Independent)

GREAT GIFT IDEAS

FOR THE SPORTS

LOVER IN YOUR LIFE!

'Hugely enjoyable, in the best tradition of British comic writing'
(Evening Chronicle)

'Light hearted entertainment ... very readable.'
(Golf World)

PUBLISHING HOUSE, TRINITY PLACE, BARNSTAPLE, DEVON EX32 9HJ   TEL: 01271 328892

'How YOU Can Beat Your Irritable Bowel Syndrome'

If you suffer from irritable bowel syndrome (IBS) you will know only too well just how much IBS can affect your life. Thousands of readers have already benefited from Vernon Coleman's advice in his book **Relief from IBS**. The advice he gives is easy to follow and includes a series of simple, practical tips designed to help you deal with IBS effectively and permanently. As with all Dr Coleman's books many readers have written to say how valuable they have found this book. *'I wish to thank you for your quite wonderful book which I fervently wish I had read years ago,'* wrote J.C. of Port Erin. *'I've just finished your book on IBS and found it helpful and instructive,'* wrote Mrs W of Devon

Relief from IBS £9.95 paperback

'Do You Want To Control Your Blood Pressure Without Pills?'

High blood pressure is a major cause of heart disease and strokes. But it can, in many cases, be controlled without the use of drugs or other outside aids. Dr Coleman's book, **High Blood Pressure**, is packed with easy to follow tips and includes simple, practical information designed to help you deal with your high blood pressure. Contents include: 'Factors which affect high blood pressure', 'When does high blood pressure need treatment?', 'Is high blood pressure a permanent problem?', 'Does high blood pressure affect life expectancy?', 'Reducing stress and learning to relax', 'Blood pressure control programme', 'Foods to eat and foods to avoid', and much, much more.

"I took your advice a few months ago and, with the help of my doctor, my blood pressure is now normal. I think that the advice you give is very sound" **P.W of Essex**

High Blood Pressure £9.95 paperback

'I Had Terrible Arthritis. I Changed My Diet. Now, My Symptoms Are Gone.'

If you suffer from arthritis you will know only too well how it can affect your life. But there are many things you can do to help overcome the symptoms of arthritis. **How to Conquer Arthritis** contains all the information you're likely to need, including: 'Getting the best out of drugs', 'Controlling pain', 'Diet and arthritis', 'Helpful alternative treatments', 'What doctors can do'. The advice in Dr Coleman's book is easy to follow and includes a series of simple, practical tips designed to help eradicate or control the symptoms of arthritis.

How to Conquer Arthritis £9.95 paperback

PUBLISHING HOUSE, TRINITY PLACE, BARNSTAPLE, DEVON EX32 9HJ   TEL: 01271 328892